AMERICA'S STORY

Historical Sources on Immigration to the United States, 1820–1924

CHET'LA SEBREE AND REBECCA STEFOFF

Cavendish Square
New York

Published in 2020 by Cavendish Square Publishing, LLC
243 5th Avenue, Suite 136, New York, NY 10016

First Edition

Cataloging-in-Publication Data

Names: Sebree, Chet'la. | Stefoff, Rebecca.
Title: Historical sources on immigration to the United States, 1820-1924 / Chet'la Sebree and Rebecca Stefoff.
Description: New York : Cavendish Square, 2020. | Series: America's story | Includes glossary and index.
Identifiers: ISBN 9781502640802 (pbk.) | ISBN 9781502640819 (library bound) | ISBN 9781502640826 (ebook)
Subjects: LCSH: Immigrants--United States--History--Juvenile literature. | United States--Emigration and immigration--History--Juvenile literature.
Classification: LCC E184.A1 S45 2019 | DDC 304.80973--dc23

Editorial Director: David McNamara
Copy Editor: Nathan Heidelberger
Associate Art Director: Alan Sliwinski
Designer: Christina Shults
Production Coordinator: Karol Szymczuk
Photo Research: J8 Media

The photographs in this book are used by permission and through the courtesy of:
Cover Library of Congress/Wikimedia Commons/File:Mulberry Street NYC c1900 LOC 3g04637u edit.jpg/Public Domain, (background and used throughout) Foxstudio/Shutterstock.com; p. 4, 77, 82 Bettmann/Getty Images; p. 8 Archive Photos/Getty Images; p. 13, 25, 65, 87, 101, 122 Everett Historical/Shutterstock.com; p. 16 Universal History Archive/Getty Images; p. 22 MPI/Getty Images; p. 29, 55 Fotosearch/Getty Images; p. 32, 79 Buyenlarge/Getty Images; p. 41 Marie Hansen-Taylor/Wikimedia Commons/File:Bayard Taylor, 1877.jpg/Public Domain; p. 43, 110 Library of Congress; p. 49 Hoover Institution/Wikimedia Commons/File:Abram Piatt Andrew, 1920.jpg/Public Domain; p. 52 George Rinhart/Corbis/Getty Images; p. 61 University of Iowa Libraries Special Collections Department/Wikimedia Commons/File:TheMeltingpot1.jpg/Public Domain; p. 68 NARA/Wikimedia Commons/File:Letter of transmittal returning files to the Commissioner of Immigration at Ellis Island. NARA 278515.tif/Public Domain; p. 70 NIH/Wikimedia Commons/File:Health Inspection of Immigrants inthe 19th Century (7844851684).jpg/CC BY SA 2.0; p. 85 The Print Collector/Getty Images; p. 92 Meyers Konversationslexikon/Wikimedia Commons/File:Dampfschiff Frisia 01.jpg/Public Domain; p. 96 Universal History Archive/UIG/Getty Images; p. 98 Bergen Public Library Norway/Wikimedia Commons/File:Ole Bull portrait (4711691694).jpg/Public Domain; p. 105 John Joergen Kanberg/Library of Congress/Corbis/VCG/Getty Images; p. 114 FPG/Getty Images; p. 129 Corbis/Getty Images; p. 131 Drew Angerer/Getty Images.

Printed in the United States of America

AMERICA'S STORY

CONTENTS

Often, families immigrated to the United States together. A Czech-Slovak family is featured here. They came to the United States through Ellis Island, an immigration station in New York.

Primary Sources

In this book, you will hear from many different people who immigrated to the United States, or came to the country from somewhere else with the goal of living there. These selections will vary in length. You'll find many easy to understand at first reading, but some may require several readings. All the selections have one thing in common, however. They are primary sources. They are important to us because they are the core material for all historical investigation.

What Is a Primary Source?

The term "primary source" is the name historians give to the information that makes up the record of human existence. A primary source is "history" itself. Primary sources are evidence. They give historians the all-important clues they need to understand the past.

HISTORICAL SOURCES ON IMMIGRATION TO THE UNITED STATES, 1820–1924

Perhaps you have read a detective story in which the detective must solve a mystery by piecing together bits of evidence he or she uncovers. The detective makes deductions, or educated guesses, based on the evidence, and solves the mystery once all the deductions point in a certain way. Historians work in much the same manner. Like detectives, historians analyze the data by careful reading and rereading. After much analysis, historians draw conclusions about an event, a person, or an entire era. Historians may analyze the same evidence and come to different conclusions. This is why there are often disagreements about an event.

Primary sources are also called documents. It is a rather dry word to describe what can be just about anything: an official speech by a government leader, an old map, an act of Congress, a letter, a diary entry, a newspaper article, a song, a poster, a cartoon, a photograph, or someone captured on tape or film.

By examining the following primary sources, you will be taking on the role of historian. Here is your chance to jump into a time period that forever changed the United States. In this book, you'll examine the great wave of immigration that swept into the country between 1820 and 1924. This century of immigration brought millions of new citizens to the United States. They came from dozens of countries around the world, bringing languages, beliefs, customs, and memories that in time became part of the United States' shared cultural landscape.

Many of these immigrants, or those who immigrated, recorded their experiences and thoughts. You'll hear from men, women, and children who made long, difficult journeys to the United States. You'll also discover what they found when they arrived. You'll hear from the Americans who welcomed immigrants and from those who feared them—from lawmakers, journalists, and ordinary citizens on both sides of the great immigration debate.

How to Read a Primary Source

Each document in this book deals with some aspect of immigration between 1820 and 1924. All of these documents help us understand what it was like to live during the century of immigration. It is important to note that our language has changed since the nineteenth and early twentieth centuries. Some words and expressions will be unfamiliar to us now. Even familiar words may have been spelled differently then. Additionally, some of the primary sources in this book were written by people who were still learning English, and others have been translated from the immigrants' native languages. Don't be discouraged! Trying to figure out language is exactly the kind of work a historian does. Like a historian, you will end up with a deeper, more meaningful understanding of the past.

As you read each document, ask yourself some basic questions. Who is writing or speaking? Who is that person's audience? What is the writer's point of view? What is he or she trying to tell the audience? Is the message clearly expressed, or is it implied (that is, stated indirectly)? What words does the writer use to convey his or her message? Are the words emotional or objective in tone? These are questions that can help you think critically about a primary source.

There are also some tools in each chapter to help you unpack these documents. Some terms and concepts you may not be familiar with have been explained in sidebars. Also, questions follow each of the documents to help you focus and think through the primary source you have just read. As you read each selection, you'll probably come up with many questions of your own. That's great! The work of a historian always leads to many, many questions. Some can be answered; others cannot and require further investigation.

Immigrants used to tip their hats in celebration at the first sight of the Statue of Liberty and Ellis Island. They knew that their new lives would be starting soon in this new country.

INTRODUCTION

A Century of Immigration

In a 1938 speech, President Franklin Delano Roosevelt encouraged listeners to "remember always that all of us ... are descended from immigrants and revolutionists." He was a descendant of both revolutionists, or American colonists who founded the United States, and Scottish immigrants. In his speech, Roosevelt encouraged people to remember that everyone in America came from someplace else or descended from people who came from someplace else. Even the Native Americans, whom we consider the original inhabitants of this country, came from Asia thousands of years ago. When we talk about immigration, though, we aren't usually referring to ancient migrations. We're usually talking about people who have come voluntarily to the United States from around the world in recent historical times.

Early American Immigration

Immigration before 1820 is not very well documented. Historians have had to piece together an account of it by drawing on many primary sources. They have used letters and diaries, population counts of cities and towns, lists of ships' passengers, and the incomplete records of the British North American colonies and later of the states.

These sources reveal that in 1775, when the American colonies began their fight for independence from Great Britain, the colonies' total population was highly diverse. For instance, nearly one-fifth of the population consisted of people from African countries. These individuals, however, are not usually called immigrants because they were enslaved. European colonists and slave traders brought these enslaved Africans to the United States against their will.

The colonial population also included people from nearly every part of Europe, as well as a few Pacific Islands and countries in Asia. The largest national group among the colonists, however, was English. They dominated the ethnic makeup of the thirteen colonies along with people from Scotland, Ireland, and Wales. Germans formed the largest non-British group, followed by the Dutch, Swedes, and French.

In 1820, however, the US government began keeping records of immigrant arrivals at American seaports. A little more than a hundred years later, a new federal law limited the number of immigrants who could enter the country. During the century between those two events, approximately forty million immigrants legally entered the United States.

Early American Opinions

Once the United States had gained its independence, it had to decide what to do about immigration. From the start, Americans held two opposing views on the subject. The inclusive or open view welcomed a wide range of newcomers and placed few barriers in their way. Perhaps some of those who held this view were immigrants. Perhaps some held this view because they remembered that their parents or grandparents had been immigrants. Others who held this view may have felt that the new nation needed the labor and energy of immigrants. They hoped immigrants would help to tame the country's wildernesses, build its cities, work in its shops and factories, and populate its enormous landscapes. Meanwhile, others held religious or political principles of equality that made them feel the United States should be open to all. Among these was Jonathan Trumbull, governor of Connecticut, who wrote in a 1782 letter:

> Our interests and our laws teach us to receive strangers, from every quarter of the globe, with open arms. The poor, the unfortunate, the oppressed from every country, will find here a ready asylum; and by uniting their interests with ours, enjoy in common with us, all the blessings of liberty and plenty. Neither difference of nation, of language, of manners, or of religion, will lessen the cordiality of their reception, among a people whose religion teaches them to regard all mankind as their brethren.

In other words, Trumbull believed that immigrants, regardless of their cultures, languages, and religions, should be welcomed. He thought the Christian faith required all people in the United States to treat immigrants as their new family.

George Washington, the new nation's first president, sometimes expressed concerns about immigrants' loyalty. However, for the most part, he held the open view. He once told some immigrants newly arrived from Ireland, "The bosom of America is open to receive not only the Opulent [wealthy] and respectable Stranger but the oppressed and persecuted of all Nations and Religions." Washington, like Trumbull, believed all, rich and poor, deserved to be welcomed into the United States.

However, his fellow Founding Fathers Benjamin Franklin and Thomas Jefferson feared allowing large numbers of non-English foreigners into the country. They were concerned that newcomers speaking their own languages, following their own customs, and living in their own communities would threaten national unity. They held an exclusive or closed view of immigration. In this view, people saw a need to limit and control entry into the country. They only wanted to admit "desirable" foreigners. Often these "desirable" immigrants were those who were wealthy and from western European countries.

That view was shared by John Jay, the first chief justice of the US Supreme Court. In 1787, he wrote that the United States was and should remain "one united people—a people descended from the same ancestors, speaking the same language, professing the same religion, attached to the same principles of government." In other words, he only wanted people from certain European countries to be able to immigrate to the United States.

During the first century of mass immigration to the United States, conflicting ideas about immigration shaped the laws and public policies. These laws determined who could enter the country and how they would be treated. But the views of Americans are only half of the story of immigration. Equally important are the

The Irish Potato Famine lasted from 1845 to 1849. It occurred when a disease destroyed the potato crops. It led to a period of starvation in Ireland. The famine was the worst one in Europe in the nineteenth century.

reasons, thoughts, and experiences of the emigrants, or people who left their homelands to come to the United States.

Reasons for Immigration

People emigrated, or left their home countries, for a variety of reasons. Many who emigrated between 1820 and 1924 were driven by economic reasons. Their reasons were similar to those who had come to the American colonies in the seventeenth and eighteenth centuries. Quite simply, they wanted a better life for themselves and their children. They believed they could have these better lives in the United States. That dream often took the form of owning land. In some countries, such as Norway, there was simply no more farmland available. In others, such as England, wealthy landowners owned or were buying up all the land. This meant that the average person could only rent the land or serve as a hired farmhand. Some emigrants hoped to earn better wages in America's growing cities than they could earn at home. Others were drawn to the United States by tales of the country's rich natural resources. There were stories about waters full of fish, soil so rich it barely needed to be tilled, and western mountains full of gold.

Emigrants also came to the United States in search of political or religious freedom. Many Europeans hoped to live in a democracy. This desire only increased after the failure of revolutionary movements that had tried to bring democracy to Europe in the 1840s. Others, such as the Jews who left eastern Europe and Russia, wanted to escape religious or ethnic persecution, or the poor treatment of someone for religious, racial, or political reasons.

Others were pushed out of their homelands by harsh circumstances. For instance, a plant disease destroyed Ireland's potato crop between 1845 and 1849. Approximately one million people died of starvation and starvation-related illnesses. Meanwhile, nearly two million emigrated to escape the famine. Another example is the Taiping Rebellion that began in southern

China in the 1850s. The period of social unrest brought chaos and poverty to the country, which drove many Chinese to immigrate to California.

Whether they were pulled to the glorious vision of America or driven from their native countries, all of the immigrants who entered the United States faced challenges. They had to leave home, make a long and generally uncomfortable journey, and then establish themselves in a new, strange land. Those events left their marks on all of them, although each experienced the challenges in a unique way.

Fortunately, many immigrants recorded at least part of their experience in letters, journals, or memoirs. Other immigrants' stories were gathered, sometimes decades later, by historians. These valuable primary sources are part of the nation's history. They are also human adventures: touching, inspiring, sorrowful, and always individual.

Each immigrant has his or her own story, triumphant or tragic. These stories tell of hard work, victories, and humiliations. Above all, they tell a story about the constant challenge of adjusting old ways and expectations to the sometimes surprising realities of life in the United States.

George Washington (*center*) was a commander for the newly formed United States during the American Revolution.

1

Immigration and Naturalization Laws

Before the American Revolution, each colony had some ability to set its own standards and rules for immigration and also for naturalization, the process by which an immigrant becomes a citizen in the eyes of the law. Some colonies passed laws designed to prevent criminals or the very poor from settling in them. Others created laws to admit only members of particular religions. The government of Great Britain, however, controlled the colonies and could make laws that applied to all of them. It did so with the Naturalization Act of 1740. Under this law, immigrants who had come to the colonies from anywhere in Europe could become British citizens after they had lived in the colonies for seven years. In 1774, frustrations among the colonists intensified when Great Britain outlawed all immigration to the colonies.

New Laws in the New Country

In 1790, the newly independent United States passed its first national immigration law. The law didn't limit immigration, but it did specify that only certain immigrants could become US citizens.

The decades that followed brought a series of immigration laws. Some of these laws changed the terms under which immigrants could become naturalized citizens. Others tried to control the conditions under which immigrants traveled. For example, the Steerage Act of 1819 said that each immigrant aboard a ship must have a certain amount of space, food, and water. Steerage was the part of the ship for passengers with the lowest-priced tickets. It was often overcrowded, with poor living conditions. On one hand, the Steerage Act of 1819 could have protected immigrants by improving shipboard conditions, which were often terrible. On the other hand, by reducing crowding, the act could also have reduced the total number of immigrants. In the end, it didn't matter. It and other steerage acts, both American and British, were almost never enforced.

Many immigration laws hoped to limit immigration into the United States by excluding certain kinds of people. The categories of people who were excluded changed over time, reflecting the changing fears of the American public and its lawmakers. After the first large-scale immigration by Asians in the mid-nineteenth century, prejudice, or opinion or bias not based in fact, led to a number of laws against Chinese immigration. Other laws later banned immigration from Japan, India, and many other parts of Asia. An 1882 law said that criminals and insane people could not enter the country. Years later, political extremists called anarchists, who did not believe in authority, carried out assassinations, or politically motivated murders, and acts of violence in the United States and other countries. After these occurrences, a new US immigration law excluded anarchists from entering the country. Later laws were also aimed at keeping anarchists and others the government viewed as potential troublemakers out of the country.

The 1917 Immigration Act set a literacy standard. Only immigrants who could read, in any language, were allowed to enter.

The Johnson-Reed Act, or the Immigration Act of 1924

The Immigration Act of 1924 took a different approach. It set a numerical limit on the total number of immigrants who could enter the country each year. It also set a quota, or specific limit, for the number of immigrants who could come from each nation. A similar "quota law" had passed three years earlier, but the 1924 law was stricter.

Its effect was immediate and dramatic. The total number of people who immigrated to the United States in 1924 was 709,896. The following year, after the new law took effect, it dropped to 294,314. The first century of mass immigration was over.

An Early Citizenship Law

On March 26, 1790, the United States Congress approved the country's first national immigration law: the Naturalization Act of 1790. Strictly speaking, it was a naturalization law rather than an immigration law. It did not spell out who could enter the United States, but it did define who could become a US citizen.

> Section 1
> Be it enacted by the Senate and House of Representatives of the United States of America in Congress assembled, That any alien, being a free white person, who shall have resided within the limits and under the jurisdiction of the United States for the term of two years, may be admitted to become a citizen thereof, on application to any common law court of record, in any one of the states wherein he shall have resided for the term of one year at least,

and making proof to the satisfaction of such court, that he is a person of good character, and taking the oath or affirmation prescribed by law, to support the constitution of the United States, which oath or affirmation such court shall administer; and the clerk of such court shall record such application, and the proceedings thereon; and thereupon such person shall be considered as a citizen of the United States. And the children of such persons so naturalized, dwelling within the United States, being under the age of twenty-one years at the time of such naturalization, shall also be considered as citizens of the United States. And the children of citizens of the United States that may be born beyond sea, or out of the limits of the United States, shall be considered as natural born citizens: Provided, That the right of citizenship shall not descend to persons whose fathers have never been resident in the United States: Provided also, That no person heretofore proscribed by any state, shall be admitted a citizen as aforesaid, except by an act of the legislature of the state in which such person was proscribed.

—Reprinted in Dennis Wepman, *Immigration: From the Founding of Virginia to the Closing of Ellis Island* (New York: Facts On File, 2002).

CONSIDER THIS

1. Who was allowed to become a citizen under the act? Who was not allowed?
2. Does the language of the act make it clear whether women could become naturalized citizens?

KEY TERMS AND CONCEPTS

From the Naturalization Act of 1790:

alien A dated, now offensive term for a foreigner or an undocumented immigrant.

be it enacted To make a bill or law.

heretofore Before now.

proscribed Banned or outlawed.

From the Chinese Exclusion Act:

locality An area or neighborhood.

misdemeanor A minor crime.

repealed Revoked or made void.

1882: The Chinese Exclusion Act Shuts the Door

During the 1870s, Americans became increasingly concerned about the growing number of immigrants from China. Some US citizens disliked the fact that Chinese immigrants competed with other laborers for jobs. These Chinese immigrants were often hired because they were willing to work for lower wages than others in the labor market. Other critics simply feared that Asian immigrants would weaken or undermine America's identity, which they saw as white, Christian, and of European descent.

Feelings against Chinese immigrants were especially strong in California and other western states, where most of the Asian newcomers had arrived. Anti-Chinese riots raged in some western

In this 1882 political cartoon, a Chinese man hangs from a branch labeled "Freedom to All." The tiger represents Irish workers and the elephant represents the Republican members of Congress who passed the Chinese Exclusion Act.

cities. In 1882, Congress responded by passing a law that banned immigration of Chinese laborers for ten years.

> Whereas, in the opinion of the Government of the United States the coming of Chinese laborers to this country endangers the good order of certain localities within the territory thereof: Therefore,
>
> Be it enacted by the Senate and House of Representatives of the United States of America in Congress assembled, That from and after the expiration of ninety days next after the passage of this act, and until the expiration of ten years after the passage of this act, the coming of Chinese laborers to the United States be, and the same is hereby, suspended; and during such suspension it shall not be lawful for any Chinese laborer to come, or, having so come after the expiration of said ninety days, to remain within the United States.
>
> Section 2
> That the master of any vessel who shall knowingly bring within the United States on such vessel, and land or permit to be landed, any Chinese laborer, from any foreign port or place, shall be deemed guilty of a misdemeanor, and on conviction thereof shall be punished by a fine of not more than five hundreds dollars for each and every such Chinese laborer so brought, and may also be imprisoned for a term not exceeding one year …
>
> Section 14
> That hereafter no State court or court of the United

States shall admit Chinese to citizenship; and all laws in conflict with this act are hereby repealed ...

That the words "Chinese laborers," whenever used in this act, shall be constructed to mean both skilled and unskilled laborers and Chinese employed in mining.

—Reprinted in Dennis Wepman, *Immigration: From the Founding of Virginia to the Closing of Ellis Island* (New York: Facts On File, 2002).

CONSIDER THIS

1. What freedoms did the Chinese Exclusion Act take away from Chinese people?
2. Does the act include any mechanisms to discourage Chinese immigration? If so, what are they?

Theodore Roosevelt's Plea to Congress

Despite some people's concerns, many Americans were in favor of immigration. Some people, however, were only in favor of the "right" kinds of immigrants entering the country. On December 3, 1901, President Theodore Roosevelt expressed this view in his annual address to Congress. He argued that the United States needed to keep out poor, ignorant, and immoral immigrants. He also wanted to keep out those he considered politically dangerous.

Less than two months prior to this speech, Roosevelt became president when President William McKinley was assassinated by American anarchist Leon Czolgosz. Roosevelt was McKinley's vice president.

Theodore Roosevelt was the twenty-sixth president of the United States. He was opposed to uneducated and poor immigrants coming into the country.

First, we should aim to exclude absolutely not only all persons who are known to be believers in anarchistic principles or members of anarchistic societies, but also all persons who are of a low moral tendency or unsavory reputation … The second object of a proper immigration law ought to be to secure by a careful and not merely perfunctory educational test some intelligent capacity to appreciate American institutions and act sanely as American citizens … Finally, all persons should be excluded who are below a certain standard of economic fitness to enter our industrial field as competitors with American labor. There should be a proper proof of personal capacity to earn an American living and enough money to insure a decent start under American conditions. This would stop the influx of cheap labor, and the resulting competition which gives rise to so much of bitterness in American industrial life, and it would dry up the springs of the pestilential social conditions in our great cities, where anarchistic organizations have their greatest possibility of growth.

Both the educational and the economic tests in a wise immigration law should be designed to protect and elevate the general body politic and social.

—Reprinted in Dennis Wepman, *Immigration: From the Founding of Virginia to the Closing of Ellis Island* (New York: Facts On File, 2002).

CONSIDER THIS

1. What kinds of tests did Roosevelt want to see applied to would-be immigrants?
2. Would these tests have favored some ethnic groups over others?
3. Do you think Roosevelt's proposals were fair?

KEY TERMS AND CONCEPTS

From Theodore Roosevelt's congressional address:

anarchistic Related to anarchy, a political philosophy that opposes all forms of organized government.

body politic Citizens.

economic fitness Financial position and earning potential.

perfunctory Basic.

pestilential Widespread and problematic, or annoying.

From the Johnson-Reed Act of 1924:

ascertained Made sure of.

attributable Can be ascribed, or attributed, to.

census An official record of a population.

fiscal year A year marked for accounting or tax purposes.

per centum Percent.

The Impact of the Johnson-Reed Act

In 1924, Congress passed the Johnson-Reed Act, sometimes called the Immigration Act of 1924. This law drastically limited the number of immigrants allowed to enter the country each year. It cut total immigration by more than 50 percent, from more than 700,000 people to fewer than 300,000 in a year. By 1927, only around 150,000 immigrants entered the United States.

The act also introduced a new and complicated system of national quotas. Each country was given a maximum number of people who could immigrate to the United States each year. These quotas reflected the existing US population. That meant that the number of people who could immigrate from each country was based on the number of people of that national background already in the United States. The nearby nations of Canada and Mexico, along with the countries of Central and South America, were not included in the quota system. The US government feared angering its neighbors by limiting immigration from them.

As far as the rest of the world went, however, the purpose of the new act was clear. The existing US population was largely of British, German, and Scandinavian ancestry, or ethnic descent. The act allowed far more immigrants from those countries than others. For instance, the act allowed only a small number of people to emigrate from Asia, Africa, and the Pacific islands.

> Section 11
> (a) The annual numerical quota of any nationality shall be 2 per centum of the number of foreign-born individuals of such nationality resident in continental United States as determined by the

IF THEY SHOULD COME BACK, VIA ELLIS ISLAND

U. S.:—"You're a Cheap Bunch of Soreheads and you Can't Land Here."

Even before the Johnson-Reed Act, Americans were resistant to immigration. This 1913 political cartoon depicts how certain people were not welcome in the United States. For instance, anyone considered a political revolutionary, like Jesus Christ and Founding Fathers like Thomas Jefferson and Benjamin Franklin, was not welcome according to this cartoon.

United States census of 1890, but the minimum quota of any nationality shall be 100.

(b) The annual quota of any nationality for the fiscal year beginning July 1, 1927, and for each fiscal year thereafter, shall be a number which bears the same ratio to 150,000 as the number of inhabitants in continental United States in 1920 having that national origin … bears to the number of inhabitants in continental United States in 1920, but the minimum quota of any nationality shall be 100.

(c) For the purpose of subdivision (b) national origin shall be ascertained by determining as nearly as may be … the number of inhabitants in the continental United States in 1920 whose origin by birth or ancestry is attributable to such geographic area. Such determination shall not be made by tracing the ancestors or descendants of particular individuals, but shall be based upon statistics of immigration and emigration, together with rates of increase of population … and such other data as may be found to bc reliable.

—Reprinted in Dennis Wepman, *Immigration: From the Founding of Virginia to the Closing of Ellis Island* (New York: Facts On File, 2002).

CONSIDER THIS

1. What kind of message about the United States did the Johnson-Reed Act send to the other nations of the world?

Laws Reflect the Times

Largely, the attitudes of Americans influenced the decisions the government made about immigration laws during this period. For instance, the development of the Chinese Exclusion Act reflected Californians' frustrations with Chinese laborers. While some people were obviously opposed to immigration and certain groups of people, attitudes about immigration varied widely.

In 1876, at the hundred-year celebration of the United States' independence from Great Britain, the torch and arm of the Statue of Liberty were displayed in Philadelphia. The statue was officially opened and dedicated in 1886.

2

American Opinions of Immigration

During the one-hundredth anniversary of the dedication of the Statue of Liberty in 1986, New York governor Mario Cuomo described what the statue had meant to his mother. His mother arrived in the United States as an immigrant. "My mother came here by ship from Italy," he said, "and her first glimpse of this great country was when she sighted the Lady of Opportunity, steadfastly lifting her torch. My mother understood immediately the meaning of that beautiful symbol … Lady Liberty said, 'Welcome. You are welcome, and the culture you bring with you is welcome, to blend with all the others into this beautiful mosaic that is America.'"

A Warm Welcome

The Statue of Liberty, also known as Lady Liberty, stands on a small island in New York Harbor. The statue of a woman holding a torch and a tablet is 305 feet (93 meters) tall with its pedestal. The monument was a gift from France to celebrate the founding of the United States. From the start, it was a symbol not just of the United States but of immigration to America.

A plaque attached to the statue's base was inscribed with the words of "The New Colossus," a poem Emma Lazarus wrote in 1883. In the poem, Lazarus compares Lady Liberty to the Colossus of Rhodes, a giant statue said to have straddled the harbor of the Greek island of Rhodes in ancient times. Lazarus identifies the Statue of Liberty as the "Mother of Exiles," or the protector of people forced to leave their countries. Lazarus sees the statue as someone who raises a light of "world-wide welcome." She writes to the Old World beyond the ocean:

> Give me your tired, your poor,
> Your huddled masses yearning to breathe free,
> The wretched refuse of your teeming shore.
> Send these, the homeless, tempest-tost to me,
> I lift my lamp beside the golden door!

Some people now believe Lazarus's depiction of immigrants is limited or biased. It suggests that all immigrants were poor. However, the poem also reveals the part of the United States that saw itself as a welcoming new home for people from around the world.

Other Sentiments

Another poem written just one year earlier shows another view. Thomas Bailey Aldrich was the editor of a widely read magazine called the *Atlantic Monthly*. In 1882, he published "Unguarded Gates" in the magazine. The poem warns that the nation's open immigration policy was letting "a wild motley throng," or a wildly diverse group, rush into the United States. In the poem, Aldrich sees the group as "bringing with them unknown gods and rites," "tiger passions," and "strange tongues." The poem asks, "O Liberty, white Goddess! Is it well / To leave the gates unguarded?" The gates, however, had already begun to close. Congress passed the Chinese Exclusion Act the year Aldrich's poem appeared.

Fears about immigrants grew during the 1890s. During that decade, there was a great increase in emigration from southern and eastern Europe and parts of Asia. Many Americans of British or northern European descent found these foreigners much more foreign than the earlier immigrants. Some began to fear that the immigrants would eventually overwhelm the society they knew and change it beyond recognition. The idea that Americans of northern European descent might one day be outnumbered by other kinds of people came to be called "race suicide." It was a powerful fear of many of those who spoke out against immigration in the late nineteenth and early twentieth centuries.

Nativists Present Their Policies

In the mid-1840s, nativists, people opposed to immigration, found a voice in the Native American Party. It was an anti-immigrant political organization of native-born Protestant Americans, or Christians that were not a part of the Catholic Church. They warned of the dangers of unlimited immigration. They were against giving naturalized citizens the right to vote. Although the party won some local elections in eastern states, it soon faded from the political scene. Its ideas did not disappear, however.

In the 1850s, a new nativist group arose, the American or Know-Nothing Party. Despite the difference in name, its views were much like those of the earlier Native American Party. Those ideas had been spelled out in the Native American Party's "Declaration of Principles of the Native American Convention" in 1845.

HISTORICAL SOURCES ON IMMIGRATION TO THE UNITED STATES, 1820–1924

It is an incontrovertible truth that the civil institutions of the United States of America have been seriously affected, and that they now stand in imminent peril from the rapid and enormous increase of the body of residents of foreign birth, imbued with foreign feelings, and of an ignorant and immoral character, who receive, under the present lax and unreasonable laws of naturalization, the elective franchise and the right of eligibility to political office …

The mass of foreign voters, formerly lost among the Natives of the soil, has increased from the ratio of 1 in 40 to 1 in 7! A like advance in fifteen years will leave the Native citizens a minority in their own land! Thirty years ago these strangers came by units and tens—now they swarm by thousands …

The body of adopted citizens, with foreign interests and prejudices, is annually advancing with rapid strides, in geometrical progression. Already it has acquired a control over our elections which cannot be entirely corrected, even by the wisest legislation, until the present generation shall be numbered with the past. Already it has notoriously swayed the course of national legislation, and invaded the purity of local justice. In a few years its unchecked progress would cause it to outnumber the native defenders of our rights, and would then inevitably dispossess our offspring, and its own, of the inheritance for which our fathers bled, or plunge this land of happiness and peace into the horrors of civil war.

—From "Address of the Delegates of the Native American National Convention, Assembled at

> Philadelphia, July 4, 1845, to the Citizens of the United States." Reprinted in William Dudley, ed., *Opposing Viewpoints in American History*, Vol. 1 (San Diego: Greenhaven Press, 1996).

CONSIDER THIS

1. Do any words or phrases in this statement make an especially strong emotional impact, either positive or negative? If so, which ones?
2. What specific threat do immigrants pose to the United States, according to this statement? Do you agree?

Another Approach: A Physician's Lecture

In the same year that the Native American Party met in Philadelphia, a physician and writer named Thomas L. Nichols delivered a lecture in favor of immigration in New York City. The lecture was later published. In it, Nichols argues that immigrants were not harmful to the United States. He goes further, claiming that it was America's destiny to bring about "the greatest intermingling of races," or the mixing together of races. He says that people have a right to move freely between nations.

> The right of man to emigrate from one country to another, is one which belongs to him by his own constitution and by every principle of justice. It is one which no law can alter, and no authority destroy …

> Emigration from various countries in Europe to America, producing a mixture of races, has had, and is still having, the most important influence upon the destinies of the human race. It is a principle,

laid down by every physiologist, and proved by abundant observation, that man, like other animals, is improved and brought to its highest perfection by an intermingling of the blood and qualities of various races ... The great physiological reason why Americans are superior to other nations in freedom, intelligence, and enterprize, is because that they are the offspring of the greatest intermingling of races ... The Yankees of New England would never have shown those qualities for which they have been distinguished in war and peace throughout the world had there not been mingled with the puritan English, the calculating Scotch, the warm hearted Irish, the gay and chivalric French, the steady persevering Dutch, and the transcendental Germans, for all these nations contributed to make up the New England character, before the Revolution, and ever since to influence that of the whole American people.

—Thomas L. Nichols, "Lecture on Immigration and Right of Naturalization," New York, 1845. Reprinted in William Dudley, ed., *Opposing Viewpoints in American History*, Vol. 1 (San Diego: Greenhaven Press, 1996).

CONSIDER THIS

1. Do the examples Nichols gives seem to support universal immigration and the mingling of "races"?
2. In what ways might Nichols's discussion of immigration and race seem limited?

KEY TERMS AND CONCEPTS

From the "Declaration of Principles of the Native American Convention":

dispossess To deprive.

elective franchise The right to vote.

imminent peril Immediate danger.

incontrovertible Undeniable.

notorious Well known.

From Thomas Nichols's lecture:

chivalric Courteous.

gay Lighthearted.

persevering Continuing to do something despite a degree of difficulty.

physiologist A doctor concerned with the function of the body and its parts.

transcendental Concerned with spiritual or philosophical matters.

From Bayard Taylor's book:

debased Of low moral character or quality.

depravity Wickedness or a lack of morality.

vice A bad habit or weak character.

Bayard Taylor's Opinion

Bayard Taylor was an American poet and journalist. He was a well-known travel writer during the mid-nineteenth century. His visits to many parts of the world earned him the nickname "the modern Marco Polo." (Polo was a famous Italian traveler from the 1200s.) Taylor's 1855 book about a journey through Asia contained extremely strong opinions about the "national character" of the Chinese people. Like other Americans who shared his anti-Chinese feelings, Taylor feared that the "pure Anglo-Saxon race," or white people from northwestern Europe, could be ruined by Chinese immigration.

> It is my deliberate opinion that the Chinese are, morally, the most debased people on the face of the earth. Forms of vice which in other countries are barely named, are in China so common, that they excite no comment among the natives. They constitute the surface-level, and below them there are deeps on deeps of depravity so shocking and horrible, that their character cannot even be hinted … Their touch is pollution, and, harsh as the opinion may seem, justice to our own race demands that they should not be allowed to settle on our soil.
>
> —Bayard Taylor, *A Visit to India, China, and Japan, in the Year 1853*, originally published in 1855. Quoted in Stuart Creighton Miller, *The Unwelcome Immigrant: The American Image of the Chinese, 1785–1882* (Berkeley and Los Angeles: University of California Press, 1969).

Bayard Taylor

1877

Bayard Taylor, a journalist and poet, wrote about his travels through Asia. Because of his experiences, he feared the effects of Chinese immigration.

CONSIDER THIS

1. Does it seem possible that an entire nation of people could have the worst morals in the world?
2. Do you think that there is such a thing as a national character?

A Senator's Speech: A Condemnation of the Chinese Exclusion Act

The Chinese Exclusion Act of 1882 was the first national law that significantly limited immigration. It was also the first to exclude a particular racial, national, or ethnic group. The year the act was passed, nearly 40,000 Chinese immigrants arrived in the United States, bringing the country's Chinese population to over 150,000 people.

The year after the act had gone into effect, only 8,000 Chinese immigrants arrived. Many of these people were scholars, diplomats, or businessmen, since the act prohibited laborers and farmers from coming to the United States. In 1887, immigration from China totaled fewer than a dozen people. When the act expired in 1892, Congress extended it for another ten years. Upon the next expiration, in 1902, Congress extended it indefinitely. The Chinese Exclusion Act was not repealed until 1943.

Even in the year it was originally passed, however, not all citizens and lawmakers supported it. Senator George Hoar of Massachusetts spoke out strongly against the Chinese Exclusion Act. Hoar recognized that the Chinese Exclusion Act was not simply about protecting American jobs. It also grew out of fear based on racial prejudice.

Senator George Hoar, a Republican from Massachusetts, thought the Chinese Exclusion Act was problematic. He believed racial prejudice was wrong.

HISTORICAL SOURCES ON IMMIGRATION TO THE UNITED STATES, 1820–1924

Nothing is more in conflict with the genius of American institutions than legal distinctions between individuals based upon race or upon occupation. The framers of our Constitution believed in the safety and wisdom of adherence to abstract principles. They meant that their laws should make no distinction between men except such as were required by personal conduct and character. The prejudice of race, the last of human delusions to be overcome, has been found until lately in our constitutions and statutes, and has left its hideous and ineradicable stains on our history in crimes committed by every generation … But it is reserved for us, at the present day, for the first time, to put into the public law of the world and into the national legislation of the foremost of republican nations a distinction inflicting upon a large class of men a degradation by reason of their race and by reason of their occupation …

The old race prejudice, ever fruitful of crime and of folly, has not been confined to monarchies or to the dark ages. Our own Republic and our own generation have yielded to this delusion, and have paid the terrible penalty.

—From George F. Hoar, Congressional Record, 47th Congress, 1st Session, 1882, vol. 13. Reprinted in William Dudley, ed., *Opposing Viewpoints in American History*, Vol. 2 (San Diego: Greenhaven Press, 1996).

KEY TERMS AND CONCEPTS

From Senator George Hoar's speech:

delusion An idea or belief that is maintained despite being in contradiction to something generally accepted as rational or true.

legislation Laws.

republican Describing a government with elected representatives.

statute A law.

From Senator Ellison Smith's speech:

assimilate To absorb.

asylum A shelter, particularly for those who need to leave their home countries.

unadulterated Pure, not mixed with anything.

From A. Piatt Andrew's article:

aristocracy The highest social class.

Bohemian Someone from a central European region that is now a part of the Czech Republic.

denounce To publicly declare as wrong or bad.

kindred Similar or like-minded.

CONSIDER THIS

1. According to Hoar, the writers of the Constitution wanted the law to make distinctions among people, or treat them differently, only on the basis of "personal conduct and character." What do you think he meant by this?
2. Speaking in 1882, Hoar says that his own country and his own generation have paid a "terrible penalty" because of race prejudice. To what is he referring?

"The Salvation of Our Own": Fears of Race Suicide

Many Americans had no objection to immigration, as long as the great majority of immigrants were white Protestants of British, German, Dutch, or Scandinavian origin. Roman Catholic immigrants from Ireland, however, disturbed enough Americans to give rise to the Know-Nothing movement in the 1850s. Additionally, increased immigration from southern and eastern Europe in the 1880s also brought about new fears.

Critics of immigration warned that Americans were committing "race suicide" by allowing so many foreigners to enter the country. As Congress debated whether or not to pass the Johnson-Reed Act in early 1924, Senator Ellison Smith of South Carolina echoed that warning in a speech to his fellow legislators, or lawmakers.

> I believe that our particular ideas, social, moral, religious, and political, have demonstrated, by virtue of the progress we have made and the character of people that we are, that we have the highest ideals of any member of the human family or any nation …

I think that we now have a sufficient population in our country for us to shut the door and to breed up a pure, unadulterated American citizenship. I recognize that there is a dangerous lack of distinction between people of a certain nationality and the breed of a dog … Thank God we have in America perhaps the largest percentage of any country in the world of pure unadulterated Anglo Saxon stock … It is for the preservation of that splendid stock that has characterized us that I would make this not an asylum for the oppressed of all countries, but a country to assimilate and perfect that splendid type of manhood that has made the American the foremost nation in her progress and her power, and yet the youngest of all the nations … Without offense, but with regard to the salvation of our own, let us shut the door.

—Ellison D. Smith, Congressional Record, LXV, part 6. Quoted in Dennis Wepman, *Immigration: From the Founding of Virginia to the Closing of Ellis Island* (New York: Facts On File, 2002).

CONSIDER THIS

1. What qualities does Smith think make Americans great?
2. Do you think that Smith's opinions display "the highest ideals of any member of the human family"?
3. This speech was made in 1924, not long before Hitler's rise to power in Germany and the beginning of World War II. What statements does it contain that reflect the thinking of the day?

Anglo-Saxon Prejudice

The flood of southern and eastern European immigrants didn't scare all Americans. Some saw them as simply the latest in a long line of new arrivals. These immigrants faced the same difficulties and criticisms as earlier generations and immigrants. In 1914, Harvard economics professor A. Piatt Andrew published "The Crux of the Immigration Question." In the article, Andrew argues that the new immigrants were not hurting the US culture or economy. He actually thought prejudice was the only reason Americans looked down on immigrants.

> The subject of immigration we have always with us in this country … The Pilgrims and Puritans of Massachusetts Bay were scarcely settled in their log huts before they began planning a policy of exclusion, and already in 1637 they voted to keep out those who were not members of their own religious sect … From that day to this the older immigrants and their descendants have tried to keep this country for those already here and their kindred folk. They have looked upon themselves as a kind of aristocracy, their supposed superiority being proportioned to the length of time that they and their ancestors have lived upon this continent, and each successive generation of immigrants newly arrived has tended with curious repetition to adopt the same viewpoint, to believe that the succeeding immigrants were inferior to the former in religion, habits, education, or what not, and ought to be kept out …

A. Piatt Andrew, shown here in 1920, shared Senator Hoar's sentiments about immigration. He thought prejudice hurt the US culture and economy more than immigration.

It looks as if in the eyes of some Americans the only good immigrants were the dead immigrants, and that the only opportunities for the country's development lay in the past …

It is easy to echo the cry of prejudice if you happen to be of Anglo-Saxon descent, and to assume an air of superiority and denounce the Italians, Greeks, Poles, Bohemians, and Russian Jews, as if they ranked somewhere between man and the beast, but were not yet wholly human. The same intolerant attitude of mind among the Anglo-Saxon Puritan settlers of early colonial days led to the whipping, imprisonment, banishment, and even hanging of Quakers and others of unlike religious beliefs …

There is no evidence that the newer immigrants are inferior to the old. It is only the recurrence of a groundless prejudice which makes some people fear so.

—A. Piatt Andrew, "The Crux of the Immigration Question," North American Review, June 1914. Reprinted in William Dudley, ed., *Opposing Viewpoints in American History*, Vol. 2 (San Diego: Greenhaven Press, 1996).

CONSIDER THIS

1. How does Andrew compare feelings about immigration in his own time with those in the past?
2. According to Andrew, what is the reason for criticism of immigrants?

Rising Tensions

Prejudice and the fear of race suicide among descendants of colonists would continue to grow during the century of immigration. Although large numbers of northwestern Europeans immigrated to the United States between 1820 and 1860, the following decades would see an increased diversity in immigrants trying to make the United States their new home. As diversity increased, so did the tensions.

Many Chinese immigrants worked on railroads like this one in California. It was backbreaking work, for which they were paid low wages.

3 The Melting Pot

From 1820 to 1860, five million people entered the United States, more than four million of them between 1840 and 1860. At least 90 percent of all immigrants from 1820 through 1860 were from northwestern Europe. More than half of these people were from the British Isles. A million and a half more were German. As the century of immigration continued, however, more diverse people began to arrive in the United States.

Early Immigration

Immigration during those early decades was more varied than statistics may suggest. People came to the United States from eastern Europe, the Mediterranean, and North Africa. The total immigration from these areas, however, was a tiny trickle compared to the flood of northwestern Europeans.

The largest group other than the northwestern Europeans came from China. After the discovery of gold in California in 1848, many Chinese people gathered together money to immigrate to "Gold Mountain," as they called California. They were hoping to make their fortunes. Many of them ended up working on crews that built railroads across the mountains and deserts of the West.

The Chinese immigrants were the first group of people to emigrate across the Pacific Ocean in such large numbers. As Ronald Takaki points out in the title of his 1989 history of Asian Americans, Chinese immigrants were *Strangers from a Different Shore*. The discrimination they encountered was caused in part by their skin color and their cultural differences from European Americans. Almost equally, the discrimination they faced was caused by white Americans' fears of job competition.

Immigration slowed during the early 1860s, during the American Civil War. However, after the war, immigration quickly returned to its former level. In fact, it surpassed that former level.

The New Immigration Era

The flow of people into the country in the late nineteenth and early twentieth centuries is sometimes called "the new immigration." This new wave of foreigners was more varied than ever. People from China still immigrated to the United States until the Chinese Exclusion Act of 1882 closed the door to most of them. However, Asian immigration continued with the arrival of people from Japan, Korea, and the Philippines.

Immigration from northwestern Europe also continued. In time, however, it was overshadowed by growing numbers of newcomers from Italy, Spain, Hungary, Greece, Russia, Poland, and other countries in southern and eastern Europe. More than 80 percent of European immigrants in 1907 were southern or eastern Europeans.

Emigrants from many different countries, cultural backgrounds, religions, and financial situations filled boats bound for the shores of the United States.

Arrivals from Middle Eastern countries such as Armenia, Syria, and Turkey increased. Immigration to the United States from other parts of the Americas rose as well. In the first twenty-five years of the twentieth century, more than eight hundred thousand Canadians and nearly three hundred thousand Mexicans moved to the United States. By the time the Immigration Act of 1924 ended America's first century of mass immigration, the United States had truly received new residents from all over the world.

"No Illusions": A Swiss Immigrant's Letter About the Frontier

Theodore Bost was born in Switzerland in 1834. He lived with his family for a few years in France before immigrating to the United States at the age of seventeen. He lived and worked on farms in rural New York and New Jersey. He also spent time at a Swiss-run Baptist mission in Canada before taking a job teaching French in Vermont. Just after his twentieth birthday he wrote to his parents, telling them of his ideas for his future.

> A number of young men from the mission … plan to go "far in the west" to buy a few hundred acres of land in what, back in Europe, we call America … In many ways the life of a pioneer, who has to clear the land before he can cultivate it, is terribly hard. His struggle is that of civilization against nature, of civilized people against savages in some places, and of people against wild animals almost everywhere. This struggle is terrifying, especially for people who are no longer young. As for myself, I have no illusions about its difficulties … but, after all, when one is young and vigorous and has a strong sense of where one's duty lies, one will be able to overcome the obstacles.

—Theodore Bost, 1854, in Ralph H. Bowen, ed. and trans., *A Frontier Family in Minnesota: Letters of Theodore and Sophie Bost, 1851–1920* (Minneapolis: University of Minnesota Press, 1981).

CONSIDER THIS

1. What do you think Bost meant by "what, back in Europe, we call America"?
2. How would you weigh the advantages and disadvantages of going to the frontier, as described by Bost?

"No Fear of Slavery": The Recruitment of Chinese Immigrants

A large majority of the Asians who immigrated to North America did so through labor recruiters or immigration brokers. These were businessmen whose job it was to sign up workers in countries such as China and deliver them to employers in the United States. People who emigrated often had to agree to work for a certain amount of time or had to borrow money from the recruiter to pay for their passage. To attract Chinese emigrants, recruiters spread flyers or posted signs in large coastal cities such as Hong Kong and Shanghai. These flyers called attention to the many benefits of immigrating to America. A Chinese immigration broker circulated this flyer in Hong Kong in 1862.

> To the countrymen of Au Chen! There are laborers wanted in the land of Oregon, in the United States of America. There is much inducement to go to this new country, as they have many great works there which are not in our own country. They will supply good houses and plenty of food. They will pay you $28 a

month after your arrival, and treat you considerately when you arrive. There is no fear of slavery. All is nice. The ship is now going and will take all who can pay their passage. The money required is $54. Persons having property can have it sold for them by correspondents, or borrow money of me upon security; I cannot take security on your children or your wife. Come to me in Hong-Kong and I will care for you until you start.

—Au Chen, Chinese immigration broker, quoted in Russell H. Conway, *Why the Chinese Emigrate and the Means They Adopt for the Purpose of Reaching America* (New York: Lee & Shepard, 1871). Reprinted in Dennis Wepman, *Immigration: From the Founding of Virginia to the Closing of Ellis Island* (New York: Facts On File, 2002).

CONSIDER THIS

1. If you were thinking about emigrating from China, would you trust the immigration broker?
2. Why do you think the flyer mentions slavery?

From Coast to Coast: John Tadich Crosses America

Among the "new immigrants" who entered the United States in the decades after the Civil War were many Slavs, people who spoke the Slavic languages of Russia and eastern Europe. These included Poles, Czechs, Slovaks, Russians, Bulgarians, Croats, Slovenes, and Serbs. Many of them settled in midwestern cities such as Cleveland and Chicago. Others fanned out across the West.

For instance, Slavs came to California during the gold rush, when many people moved to California after gold was discovered

KEY TERMS AND CONCEPTS

From the Chinese immigrant broker's flyer:
inducement A thing that persuades someone to do something.
security Something promised as a guarantee of repayment.

From John Tadich's account:
papoose A dated, now offensive term for a Native American child; also a term for a type of bag used to carry a child on one's back.
shanty A small, poorly constructed structure.
squaw A dated, now offensive term for a Native American wife.

in 1848. Years afterward, California continued to draw many Slavic immigrants. Like most other immigrant groups, Slavs generally moved to regions where people from their home communities or regions had already settled.

Crossing the Atlantic Ocean, however, was only the first part of their journey. John Tadich came to California from Dalmatia, an eastern European region that is now part of Croatia, in 1871. He describes the second part of the journey: traveling across the United States.

> From New York we traveled on the railroad by way of Chicago and Council Bluffs. I remember that there were no dwelling houses in Council Bluffs at that time, just a little shanty for the railroad station. We crossed the Mississippi River on a shaky wooden bridge. Omaha, too, was a small city … The train traveled so slowly that the men of the party were

becoming impatient. They were anxious to reach California and start to work; because ... they were all married men with families left in the old country ... I recall now that whenever our train would stop on a side track, hundreds of Indians and their squaws, with papooses on their backs, would gather around the trains. They were just as curious about us as we were about them.

—John V. Tadich, "The Yugoslav Colony of San Francisco on My Arrival in 1871," quoted in Vekoslav Meler, ed., *The Diamond Jubilee, 1857–1932, of the Slavonic and Benevolent Mutual Society of San Francisco* (San Francisco: The Slavonic Pioneers, 1932).

CONSIDER THIS

1. What aspects of the journey across the United States would have been new to an immigrant from eastern Europe?
2. What do you think is the connection between having a family in the old country and being eager to start work?

Israel Zangwill Coins a Term

Israel Zangwill was an English writer whose 1898 novel *The Children of the Ghetto* portrayed Jewish immigrants living in London, England. Ten years later, Zangwill turned his attention to the immigrants of America in his best-known work, a play called *The Melting Pot*. The play is about a tortured romance between two immigrants, a Jewish man (David) and a gentile, or non-Jewish, woman (Vera). Their communities hated each other in Russia,

We get the term "melting pot," meaning people from diverse backgrounds coming together in one place, from Israel Zangwill's play *The Melting Pot*.

the "old country." In the play, they come to see that love conquers hate. They also learn that, in America, immigrants can shed the burden of the past.

Zangwill called America a great crucible, a large container in which substances can be melted at high heat, or melting pot. In this melting pot, God's fire burns away old differences to create a new, united people. The image of the melting pot, of America as a place where different people blend to form a new society, became one of the most widely used metaphors for immigration. These final lines of the play are spoken as the main characters gaze from a rooftop at New York City.

VERA
Look! How beautiful the sunset is after the storm!

DAVID
[Prophetically exalted by the spectacle]

It is the fires of God round His Crucible.

[He drops her hand and looks downward]

There she lies, the great Melting-Pot—listen! Can't you hear the roaring and the bubbling? There gapes her mouth—

[He points east]

—the harbour where a thousand mammoth feeders come from the ends of the world to pour in their human freight. Ah, what a stirring and a seething! Celt and Latin, Slav and Teuton, Greek and Syrian …

KEY TERMS AND CONCEPTS

From Israel Zangwill's *The Melting Pot*:
alchemist Someone who practices alchemy, a medieval science and philosophy that aimed, among other things, to transform less valuable metals into gold.
prophetically exalted Deeply inspired.

From Jacob Riis's *The Battle with the Slum*:
Balkan peninsula A region in southern Europe that includes present-day Albania, Bosnia and Herzegovina, Bulgaria, Croatia, Greece, Macedonia, Montenegro, Romania, Serbia, Slovenia, and the European part of Turkey.
pushcart A handcart.

VERA
[Softly, nestling to him]

Jew and Gentile—

DAVID
Yes, East and West, and North and South, the palm and the pine, the pole and the equator, the crescent and the cross—how the great Alchemist melts and fuses them with his purging flame! Here shall they all unite to build the Republic of Man and

the Kingdom of God! Ah, Vera, what is the glory of Rome and Jerusalem where all nations and races come to worship and look back, compared with the glory of America, where all races and nations come to labour and look forward!

—Israel Zangwill, *The Melting Pot: Drama in Four Acts* (New York: Macmillan, 1908).

CONSIDER THIS

1. In Zangwill's view, what is the desired result of immigration?
2. Why does David think that America is more glorious than Rome and Jerusalem?
3. Do you agree with Zangwill's viewpoint that an immigrant should look forward, not back?

Jacob Riis Casts an "Unblinking Eye at the Motley Crowd"

Jacob Riis emigrated from Denmark. He became a photographer and journalist in the United States. Riis was also a crusader, or a person who campaigns for a cultural cause, for social reform, or change. His best-known book was *How the Other Half Lives* (1890). It exposed the terrible conditions of America's urban slums, or areas inhabited by poor people, especially in New York City.

Riis returned to the topic several years later in *The Battle with the Slum*. In a chapter titled "On Whom Shall We Shut the Door?" he considers the flow of "new emigrants" through the receiving station on Ellis Island in New York Harbor. Established in 1892,

Ellis Island was an immigration receiving station in the New York Harbor. Between its opening in 1892 and 1924, when the restrictive Johnson-Reed Act was passed, it was the busiest immigration station in the United States, ushering over twelve million immigrants into the country.

HISTORICAL SOURCES ON IMMIGRATION TO THE UNITED STATES, 1820–1924

Ellis Island served as a main immigration station through which immigrants crossing the Atlantic passed. Between its establishment and the passing of the Johnson-Reed Act in 1924, an estimated twelve million immigrants passed through Ellis Island.

> The Jew and the Italian have filled the landscape so far, because, as a matter of fact, that is what they do. Yesterday it was the Irishman and the Bohemian. Tomorrow it may be the Greek, who already undersells the Italian from his pushcart in the Fourth Ward, and the Syrian, who can give Greek, Italian, and Jew points at a trade. The rebellious Slovak holds his own corner in our industrial system ... From Dalmatia comes a new emigration, and there are signs that the whole Balkan peninsula has caught the fever and is waiting only for cheap transportation to be established on the Danube [River] to the Black Sea, when there is no telling what may be heading our way. I sometimes wonder what thoughts come to the eagle that perches over the great stone gateway on Ellis Island, as he watches the procession that files through it in the United States, day after day, and never ends. He looks out of his grave, unblinking eye at the motley crowd, but gives no sign ...
>
> Fear not, eagle! While that gate is open let no one bar the one you guard. While the flag flies ... keep it aloft over Ellis Island and have no misgivings.
>
> —Jacob Riis, T*he Battle with the Slum* (New York: Macmillan & Co., 1912).

CONSIDER THIS

1. Does this selection suggest that Riis is for immigration or against it?
2. How might Riis's background as an immigrant and social reformer have influenced his description of the various kinds of immigrants?

The Other Side of the Story

Although Americans had a variety of opinions about the incoming immigrants, some ignoring the fact that their ancestors emigrated, the new immigrants had their own take on the story. These people had left their home countries in hopes of a better—or at the very least, different—life. The decisions these people made to leave home, though, did not come without their difficulties.

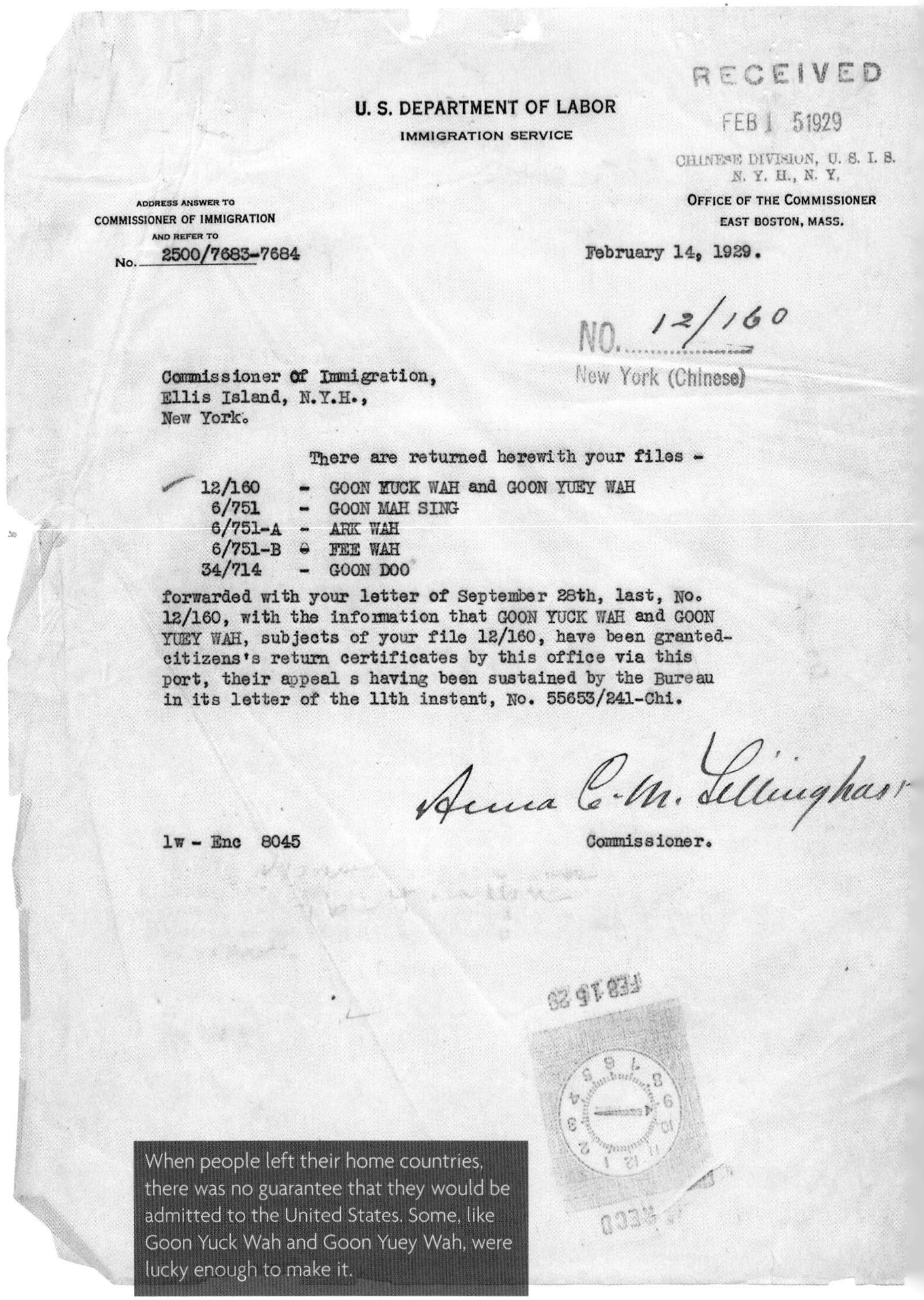

U. S. DEPARTMENT OF LABOR
IMMIGRATION SERVICE

RECEIVED
FEB 15 1929
CHINESE DIVISION, U. S. I. S.
N. Y. H., N. Y.

OFFICE OF THE COMMISSIONER
EAST BOSTON, MASS.

ADDRESS ANSWER TO
COMMISSIONER OF IMMIGRATION
AND REFER TO
No. 2500/7683-7684

February 14, 1929.

NO. 12/160
New York (Chinese)

Commissioner Of Immigration,
Ellis Island, N.Y.H.,
New York.

There are returned herewith your files -

12/160 - GOON YUCK WAH and GOON YUEY WAH
6/751 - GOON MAH SING
6/751-A - ARK WAH
6/751-B - FEE WAH
34/714 - GOON DOO

forwarded with your letter of September 28th, last, No. 12/160, with the information that GOON YUCK WAH and GOON YUEY WAH, subjects of your file 12/160, have been granted citizens's return certificates by this office via this port, their appeal s having been sustained by the Bureau in its letter of the 11th instant, No. 55653/241-Chi.

Anna C. M. Tillinghast

lw - Enc 8045

Commissioner.

FEB 15 29

REC'D

When people left their home countries, there was no guarantee that they would be admitted to the United States. Some, like Goon Yuck Wah and Goon Yuey Wah, were lucky enough to make it.

4 *Emigration*

Emigration is when someone moves from their home country in order to establish a life in a new country. People have a variety of different reasons for wanting to leave their home countries. However, many people left home to escape persecution or to embrace better opportunities.

Leaving Home

In 1922, Marge Glasgow emigrated from her home in Motherwell, Scotland. "My whole idea," she told an interviewer years later, "was to get to [the] United States, and work, and help bring my family … I had no relatives in America … It wasn't easy for me to convince my parents that I was capable of going over and taking care of myself. But I was determined … I finally got my way."

Glasgow was fifteen years old when she made the ten-day ocean crossing. Once she had arrived in America, she recalled, "I began to have regrets about leaving home. I was feeling very lonesome, sorry for myself, crying all the time." Glasgow soon adjusted to her new surroundings. However, her brush with homesickness and unhappiness was something that many immigrants experienced. Coming to America wasn't just the beginning of a new life. It also meant saying good-bye to the old life.

Some families emigrated together. While they had to say farewell to homes, friends, relatives, familiar surroundings, and beloved possessions, at least they still had each other. Often, however, one family member, like Marge Glasgow, emigrated first. These individuals hoped to earn money to send home so that the rest of their family could follow. Some families were separated for years before being reunited. Other separations were permanent.

After leaving their home countries, emigrants had to undergo rigorous inspection before entering their new home.

Tough Realities

In 1871, German immigrant Heinrich Möller wrote to his mother and father, "Dear parents! If God grants me life we will meet again before 2 years have passed, for then I will come to Germany to get you, then you will be near me." Busy with a house, farm, and growing family, Möller never made that journey. Nine years later, he wrote:

> Dearly beloved parents, I have received your letter and learned from it that your end is near, or perhaps by the time this letter reaches you, it will already be too late, I hope not since my greatest desire is to see you again, dear father, I have had no peace of mind for years now, I always think about coming back to Germany again but times have been so bad … I haven't given up all hope of seeing you again. If it is not God's will, we'll have to accept it and hope to meet if not in this world than in the next.

For many emigrants, even those most eager to reach the United States, the act of leaving home brought both sadness and joy. Even after they became established in their new homes in America, some longed to see again the places and people they had left behind. At the same time, people in the old countries eagerly awaited letters and visits from those who had emigrated. By telling of their successes in America, the land of golden opportunity, some of those who had already left home inspired others to follow in their footsteps.

A Chinese Emigrant Returns Home

Not everyone who left his or her homeland intended to stay away forever. Many emigrants simply wanted to work in America for a time and save their money. They hoped to return to their former homes able to live better than they had before. Some achieved this dream. Lee Chew, an immigrant from China, described the return of a successful emigrant to his native village in China.

> [When] I was about sixteen years of age, a man of our tribe came back from America and took ground as large as four city blocks and made a paradise of it. He put a large stone wall around and led some streams through it and built a palace and summer house and about twenty other structures ... The man had gone away from our village a poor boy. Now he returned with unlimited wealth, which he had obtained in the country of the American wizards ... Having made his wealth among the barbarians this man had faithfully returned to pour it out among his tribesmen, and he is living in our village now very happy, and a pillar of strength to the poor.
>
> —Lee Chew, "Life Story of a Chinaman," in Hamilton Holt, ed., *The Life Stories of Undistinguished Americans as Told by Themselves* (New York: James Pott & Co., 1906).

CONSIDER THIS

1. Why do you think the Chinese villagers called Americans "wizards" and "barbarians"?
2. What effect might this emigrant's return have had on Lee Chew and other villagers?

Hiraeth: Notes from a Welshman

Many emigrants felt a strong desire to tell the folks back home about their experiences. They wrote letters. If they could not read and write, they often found others to write for them. Most letters were to family members, such as this letter from a Welsh emigrant named John Lloyd to his parents in his home village.

In order to share emigrants' experiences with the largest possible number of interested readers back home, sometimes newspapers published their letters. Printed in papers or passed from hand to hand, emigrants' letters were a valuable source of information for others who were thinking about making the journey. They communicated useful, practical details. Sometimes they also prepared their readers for the emotional strains and surprises that awaited the emigrant.

> August 1, 1868
> Ha! Ha! here I am at last with my feet on the famous land of America. Many laughed at me when I said I was coming here and said, "We will believe you when you have gone." Well, will they believe me now because I have gone...
>
> Talking about going to America and actually going are two different things. Many of my friends came to see me off down the river. They looked worriedly at me and I at them. It was a shaky first step from the landing stage onto the ship. As we sailed those who were left behind waved their handkerchiefs, their hands and their hats above their heads ... Soon we could see the shores of Flintshire, and when opposite Rhyl, ah! there was the dear Clwyd Valley as if opening before me and a feeling of hiraeth came

KEY TERMS AND CONCEPTS

From John Lloyd's letter:
hiraeth The longing for a place to which you cannot return; roughly, nostalgia or homesickness.

From Catherine Moran's account:
cream of the milk The very best part.

over me as I remembered the Pont'ralltgoch lay in that direction and as I caught sight of the haunts of my youth I shed a tear.

—Quoted in Alan Conway, ed., *The Welsh in America: Letters from the Immigrants* (Minneapolis: University of Minnesota Press, 1961).

CONSIDER THIS

1. What emotions does Lloyd reveal in this part of his letter?
2. How do you think he feels about his decision to emigrate?

The Beginning of One Boy's Journey

Once they had established themselves in the United States, immigrants often sent advice and money to help family members and friends follow them. Some returned to their former homes to bring others back to America with them. John Tadich was brought as a boy to California from his home in Dalmatia. His experience shows how networks of relatives and friends aided emigrants.

> On the twenty second day of May, in the year 1871, I left my native town of Starigrad, in Dalmatia, on the beautiful eastern coast of the Adriatic Sea … Bidding farewell to my mother, I started on my long journey, my father and brother accompanying me as far as Split. We had to go first to … meet Lorenzo Nizetich, a pioneer miner of Sutter Creek, Amador County, California, who was returning to California, and whose party my uncle, Nicholas Buja (already in California) had advised me to join. We arrived at the Nizetich home about noontime and found a good lunch prepared for us. I remember well that after the lunch I went outside like any young boy would do, to play with a group of children in front of the church. The other boys were strangers to me; but they all knew that I was the boy who was going to California with Lorenzo Nizetich. One of the boys came very close to me and asked many questions about my trip to California and I recall that he said to me with sadness in his voice: "Oh, I wish I could go with you."

—John V. Tadich, "The Yugoslav Colony of San Francisco on My Arrival in 1871," quoted in Vekoslav Meler, ed., *The Diamond Jubilee, 1857–1932, of the Slavonic and Benevolent Mutual Society of San Francisco* (San Francisco: The Slavonic Pioneers, 1932).

CONSIDER THIS

1. Why might the parents of a young boy have allowed him to go to California?

Catherine Moran Moves to Boston

When eighteen-year-old Catherine Moran emigrated from Ireland to Boston in 1903, her journey was just one of many partings her family had made over the years. For instance, one of her sisters and an uncle emigrated from Ireland to Australia. This move was not uncommon. Many people who left England, Scotland, or Ireland went to other British territories, such as Australia or Canada. Some Europeans and Asians also emigrated to South American nations such as Peru, Argentina, and Uruguay. During the century of immigration, however, the United States was the chief destination of people who wanted to change their lives.

> There was twelve in our family …
>
> We wasn't put out of our land because I had brothers. Some of them were old enough to work and just pay back the rent. Just exist, try to exist.

Mrs. Thomas McKessy, pictured here, emigrated from Ireland with ten of her twenty-one children in the early twentieth century.

My mother kept house and my father had no work but just the bit of land we had, to work it, and give the cream of the milk to England for everything ...

It was only about ten dollars or somethin' to come [to the United States] at that time. It was cheap. I'm here seventy-three years. My sister's here seventy-five. Once she's here she sent for me, see. There was five of us out here ...

I came by myself, except you might meet someone on the boat was from nearby, but you wouldn't know them at home. I was eighteen in April, and I come, I think, May or June.

—Catherine Moran McNamara, interview, in June Namias, *First Generation: In the Words of Twentieth-Century American Immigrants* (Boston: Beacon Press, 1978).

CONSIDER THIS

1. Does this passage suggest why so many members of the Moran family left their homeland?
2. What might Moran have liked about living in the United States?

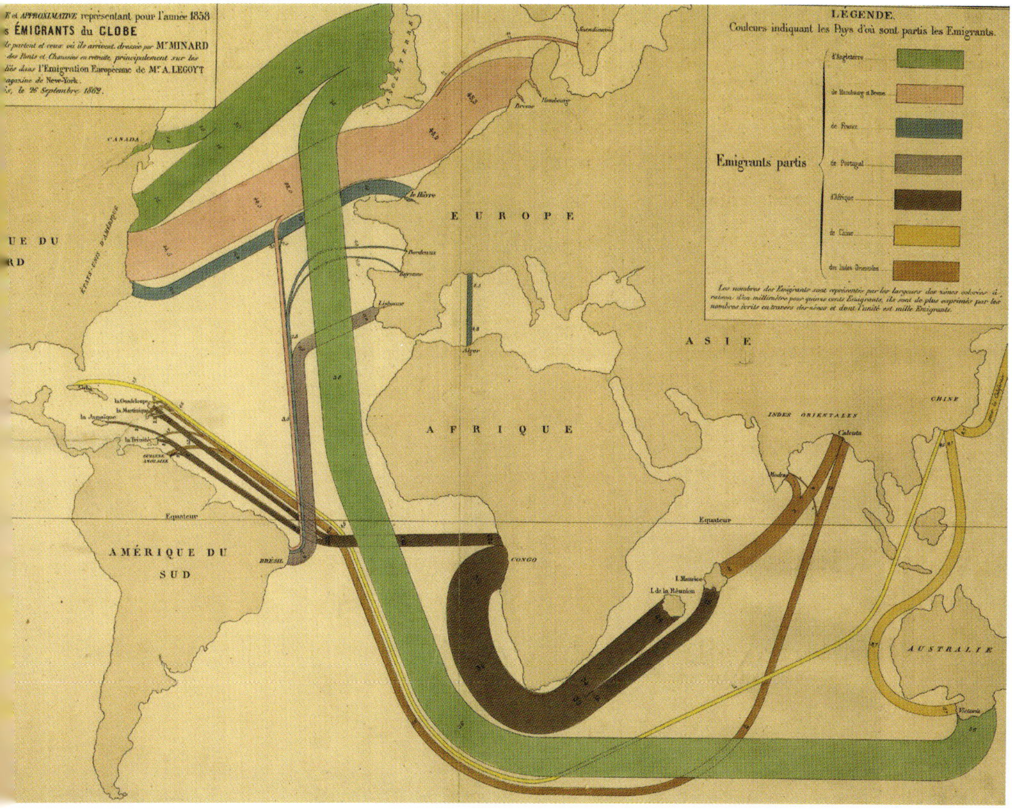

This 1862 map shows emigration patterns from England (green), Germany (pink), France (blue), Portugal (purple), Africa (dark brown), China (yellow), and India (light brown). The width of each band represents the size of the population that emigrated.

One Family's Emigration from Korea

Paik Kuang Sun was born in Korea in 1900. Five years later, after Japan began a military occupation, or the act of entering and controlling an area, of Korea that lasted for many years, the Paik family was forced from its house. Soon afterward, the Paiks left their country. Paik Kuang Sun—later known as Mary Paik—later wrote an account of her family's emigration and her life in Hawaii and California. As her story shows, some of those who came to America were driven out of their homelands by forces beyond their control.

> In 1905, … I saw two men … walking towards our house … I ran into the house to call Grandmother. She came out to meet them. After a few minutes she returned … and said that we had to move out right away … The two strange men were Japanese officers, and they wanted … to … use our home to house their soldiers …
>
> The family decided to go to Inchon, the nearest large city with a harbor …
>
> There happened to be two ships in Inchon harbor, sent by owners of sugar cane plantations … People were told that if a man signed a contract to work for one year, he and his family would be given free passage to Hawaii … His wages were to be fifty cents per day … Father signed on, and that was how we went to Hawaii …
>
> —Mary Paik Lee, *Quiet Odyssey: A Pioneer Korean Woman in America*, Sucheng Chan, ed. (Seattle: University of Washington, 1990).

CONSIDER THIS

1. Why do you think the narrator's father signed the labor contract?
2. Can you think of other examples of people driven out of their homes by invasion or occupation?

Only the First Step

Despite its emotional toll, actually packing bags and leaving home was only a small fraction of the journey. Most emigrants, aside from those emigrating from Canada and Mexico, still also needed to board a ship and cross an ocean to get to the land of opportunity. These ships, however, did not always provide the easiest passage for immigrants. Often times, the ocean passage was difficult.

This image represents the three different classes of travelers on the *Frisia*: tourist (*top*), salon (*middle*), and steerage (*bottom*). As you can see, the tourist travelers enjoyed a lot more comfort than those in steerage.

5 *Ships and Stations*

Except for those who came by land from Canada and Mexico, most arrivals to the United States during the century of immigration came by passenger ship. By the 1870s, 90 percent of immigrants arrived in the United States on steamships like the *Japan* and the *Frisia*. These ships, however, varied in their capacity and speed. For instance, the *Frisia*, a German ship built in Scotland in 1872, could carry 820 passengers. It could cross the Atlantic from Europe to the United States in twelve days. The *Japan*, however, took about a month to arrive in the United States. It was traveling a greater distance than the *Frisia*, crossing the Pacific to San Francisco. It could hold slightly over 1,000 passengers—about 200 in first class and 900 in steerage.

The Horrors of Steerage

Some could afford to travel more or less comfortably. Many emigrants, however, could barely scrape together the money to pay for the cheapest passage available. They traveled in what was known as steerage, which meant that their quarters were more crowded and less sanitary.

Despite laws meant to improve the treatment of steerage passengers, many emigrants endured miserable conditions on their way to the new country. In 1853, a group of Norwegians who had emigrated to the United States were so outraged that they wrote to a Norwegian newspaper, warning their fellow countrymen and countrywomen.

Occasionally, shipboard conditions became nightmarish. Vessels could be crowded and filthy. Outbreaks of disease among the steerage passengers could bring suffering and death. Even on easier voyages, emigrants confronted the ordinary difficulties of ocean travel, such as seasickness and storms. Although the travel could be difficult, some travelers enjoyed their first sea voyages and their first glimpses of a world larger than their village or neighborhood.

Receiving Stations

Throughout the century of immigration, the majority of immigrants arrived in New York City, the biggest harbor in the United States. To make their entry more orderly and to provide basic services such as money changing to the new arrivals, the city opened a receiving station called Castle Garden in 1855. States and cities opened similar stations in other ports, such as Boston and New Orleans. However, Castle Garden remained the busiest.

With the number of immigrants continuing to rise, the federal government took control of immigration from the states in 1891. The government established the Office of the Superintendent of

Once immigrants arrived in the United States, they then had to transport all of their worldly belongings to the immigration station. Each person was given a paper with a number they would exchange for a visa, which is a document that allows people entry into a country.

Immigration to oversee the newcomers' entry into the country. It was renamed the Bureau of Immigration in 1895. The bureau closed Castle Garden, which had become run down. It built a new federal receiving station on Ellis Island in New York Harbor, which opened in 1892. For the rest of the century of immigration, Ellis Island was the main point of entry.

The government closed it in 1954 because immigration had decreased and many of those who immigrated arrived in airplanes. Today, a museum of immigration stands on the island where once thousands of immigrants nervously awaited the inspections and formalities that would let them enter the country.

Similarly, there was a receiving station for people immigrating to the West Coast. It was called Angel Island. It was in San Francisco Bay. Angel Island, a former military base, opened in 1910 in an effort to control immigration from Asia. It remained in use until 1940.

After 1882, the Chinese Exclusion Act limited immigration from China to students and teachers, businesspeople, diplomats and other government officials, temporary visitors, and American citizens, including relatives of Chinese people who had been born in the United States. Some of those who came to the country posed as students, teachers, or sons of Chinese American citizens. Desperate to reach America, they used phony documents and memorized the details of their "families."

This preparation was necessary because they faced strict examinations at Angel Island. If the Chinese emigrants failed to convince the immigration officials that they qualified to be admitted, they would be held on Angel Island and then returned to China. The examination process itself could drag on for months.

These sorts of examination failures frightened those who were coming through both Angel and Ellis Islands. During the century of immigration, immigrants endured so much—from the horrors of steerage to stress of receiving stations—in hopes of a better life in America.

Chinese immigrants weren't the only individuals who had a hard time passing inspections at Angel Island. Here, Japanese passengers attempt to enter the United States through Angel Island after the Johnson-Reed Act was passed.

KEY TERMS AND CONCEPTS

From William Smith's book:

hogshead A large barrel.

ship-fever One of several infectious diseases that broke out on ships, including typhoid and cholera.

From Mary Antin's *The Promised Land:*

berth A bed or bunk on a ship.

fugitive sunshine Rare moments of good weather.

Polotzk Also spelled Polotsk, a city in modern-day Belarus that was previously part of Russia.

"Disastrous Voyage": A Tale from Steerage

Liverpool was one of England's major shipping ports. During the century of immigration, its ships carried hundreds of thousands of immigrants from England and all over Europe to the United States. One who made that journey was William Smith. He crossed the Atlantic between 1847 and 1848. Soon afterward, he wrote a book about his experiences. His "disastrous voyage" included, among other problems, disease aboard the ship, a serious water shortage, and bad food.

> Most of those who had died of ship-fever were delirious, some a day, others only a few hours previous to death …

When we had been at sea a month, the steward discovered the four hogsheads, by oversight or neglect, had not been filled. On the following morning ... our water was reduced from two quarts to one quart per day for an adult and one pint for a child ... I had nothing but ship allowances to subsist upon, which was scarcely sufficient to keep us from perishing, being only a pound of sea-biscuit (full of maggots) and a pint of water ... I was seized with ship-fever, at first I was so dizzy that I could not walk without danger of falling; ... my brains felt as if they were on fire, ... and my lips were parched with excessive thirst.

This disastrous voyage [came] to an end, after an absence of exactly eight weeks from the shores of my native land ... My whole lifetime did not seem so long as the last two months appeared to me.

—William Smith, *An Immigrant's Narrative; or a Voice from the Steerage* (New York: W. Smith, 1850).

CONSIDER THIS

1. Would you be willing to undergo an ordeal such as Smith's to come to America?

Mary Antin's Account of Crossing the Atlantic

In 1894, thirteen-year-old Mary Antin, her mother, and her siblings left their home in Russia to join Antin's father. He had immigrated to the United States three years earlier. Antin saw the journey as "a tremendous adventure." Later, she published autobiographical articles about her experiences in the *Atlantic Monthly*. In 1912, the articles were collected into a book called *The Promised Land*.

It described every step of Antin's journey, starting with the awe and envy of playmates in her Jewish neighborhood in the city of Polotsk when they learned that she was going to America. She wrote about the family's reunion in Boston and her thoughts about how being an immigrant had shaped her life. Here she describes boarding the ship and making the ocean voyage, which she had also described in a letter to her uncle.

> Our turn came at last. We were conducted through the gate of departure, and after some hours of bewildering manoeuvres … we found ourselves—we five frightened pilgrims from Polotzk—on the deck of a great big steamship afloat on the strange big waters of the ocean.
>
> For sixteen days the ship was our world. My letter dwells solemnly on the details of life at sea, as if afraid to cheat my uncle of the smallest circumstance. It does not shrink from describing the torments of seasickness; it notes every change in the weather. A rough night is described, when the ship pitched and rolled so that people were thrown from their berths; days and nights when we crawled through dense fogs, our foghorns drawing answering warnings from invisible ships. The perils of the sea were not minimized in the imaginations of us inexperienced voyagers. The captain and his officers ate their dinners, smoked their pipes and slept soundly in their turns, while we frightened emigrants turned our faces to the wall and awaited our watery graves.
>
> All this while the seasickness lasted. Then came happy hours on deck, with fugitive sunshine, birds atop the crested waves, band music and dancing and

> fun. I explored the ship, made friends with officers and crew, or pursued my thoughts in quiet nooks. It was my first experience of the ocean, and I was profoundly moved.
>
> —Mary Antin, *The Promised Land* (Boston and New York: Houghton Mifflin Company, 1912).

CONSIDER THIS

1. Were Antin's moods during the voyage influenced by outside forces? If so, what were those forces?
2. How do you think Antin's age might have affected how she felt about the voyage?

Aboard the *Mongolia*: Evelyn Berkowitz's Journey

Evelyn Berkowitz's family emigrated from a small town in Hungary in 1921, when she was twelve. She was old enough to be aware of conditions on the *Mongolia*, the ship that carried her family and many other immigrants.

> First of all, everybody got sick. It was rough seas. For five days I was laid up. I didn't eat a thing. I was the worst. The little ones would throw up, and then they were all right. My brother came in eating a piece of bread from the lunchroom and he said, "Oh, this piece of bread tastes awful." Next thing, he starts throwing up.
>
> There were also rats on the boat. I was on the upper bunk, and there were pipes above. And the rats were just running back and forth on those pipes. One day,

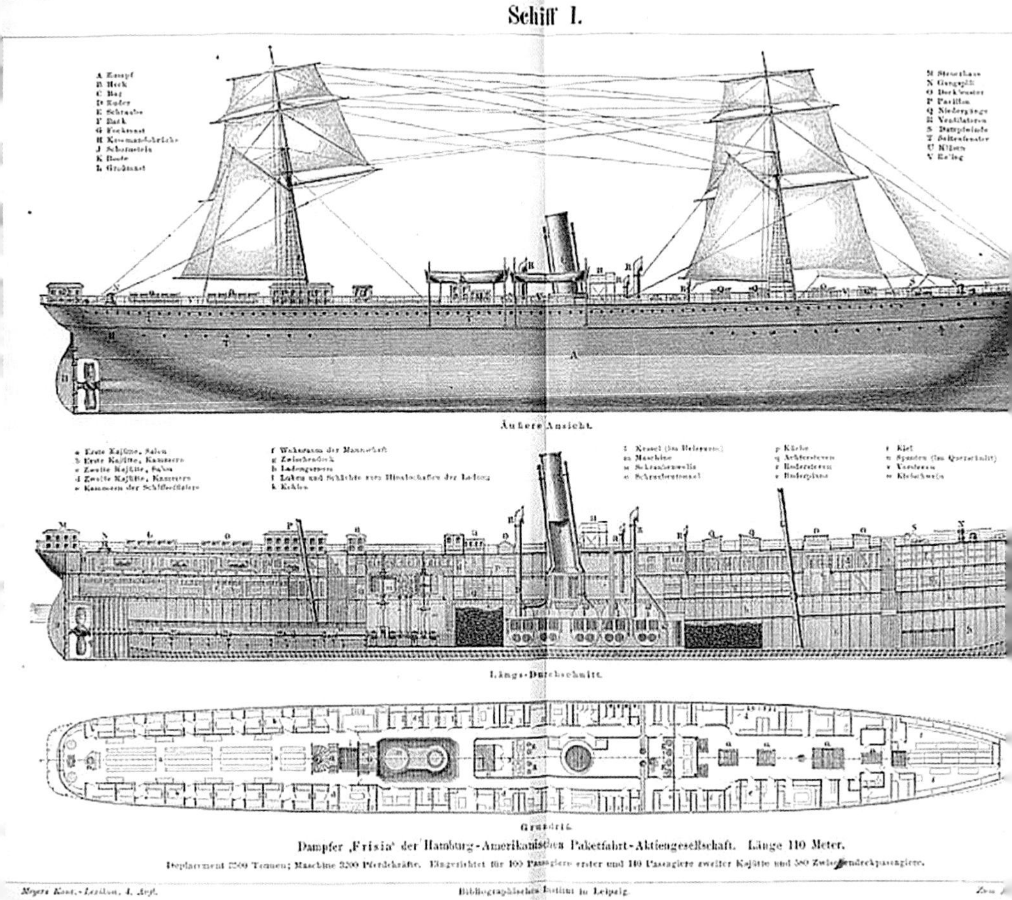

The *Frisia,* a German steamship built in Scotland, transported people immigrating to the United States from Europe.

Dad hit one on the tail, and that thing was squeaking so far. After that we got relief, because usually when they get hurt they don't come back to that same spot. It wasn't a nice boat.

Then a couple of days out, the ship sprung a hole and water was coming in. In fact, we were walking around with our life jackets. They sent an SOS out, and told us another ship was coming to help us. But before that ship got to us, they fixed the hole, and we kept on going. In New York they reported in the paper that the *Mongolia* sunk, and all the people went down. When we got to New York, they couldn't believe it. They said we were found people, that the boat went down.

We arrived in New York late December 1921. We were eleven days on ship. When we saw that Statue of Liberty, everybody started screaming and crying and hollering, they were just so happy to see it, to be in America. By this time I was feeling better and it was such a thrill to see it. Then for one week we waited in New York Harbor, because a lot of other ships had come in and we had to wait our turn.

—Evelyn Berkowitz, interview, in Peter Morton Coan, *Ellis Island Interviews: In Their Own Words* (New York: Facts On File, 1997).

CONSIDER THIS

1. Evelyn says that people in New York called the *Mongolia's* passengers "found people." What do you think this means?
2. What might Evelyn's feelings have been during the week the ship waited in the harbor?

Ellis Island Examinations

Theodore Spako was sixteen years old in 1911, when he left his home and parents to go to the United States. Years later, he told an interviewer about the journey. On the ship, he befriended Gus, a fellow Greek, and Gus's father. Like all arrivals, they faced examination on Ellis Island. Some who hoped to enter were turned away because they did not pass medical tests or other requirements. The examinations were a great source of anxiety and, for those who were refused entry, despair.

> We landed in New York after twenty-two days at sea. I remember we see Statue of Liberty. Gus ask me, "What's the statue?" And then we're looking at the statue, and his father say, "That's Christopher Columbus." And I put my two cents out. I say, "Listen, this don't look like Christopher Columbus. That's a lady out there."
>
> Everybody was hungry, and they started examinations on Ellis Island. I had twenty-five dollars in my pocket. I knew to bring money, otherwise they keep you there. They wouldn't let you go to shore without money. Because if you were hungry, you might steal. And I was alongside Gus, and noticed he had a chalk mark on his back. I couldn't reach or see my own back,

> so I asked him, "Do I have a chalk mark on the back?" So he looked, he says, "No." I say, "You've got one. Your father, too." And I'm thinking, either they go back to Greece or I go back to Greece. So what happened, the one with the chalk mark went back to Greece. Gus and his father went back. I don't know why.
>
> I just thank God. To this day I pray, dear Lord, and thank God, that I was admitted to the United States, that they didn't put a chalk mark on my back.
>
> —Theodore Spako, interview, quoted in Peter Morton Coan, *Ellis Island Interviews: In Their Own Words* (New York: Facts On File, 1997).

CONSIDER THIS

1. What could officials at Ellis Island have done differently to reduce the anxiety that Spako and other immigrants felt?
2. What could have been the reasons that Gus and his father were turned away?

A Fresh Start

Spako, for one reason or another, was spared. He, unlike Gus and his father, made it into the United States. Again, however, making it to the United States was just another step in the journey. Once people had braved the ocean and survived the voyage, they still had to do the hard work of setting up a life in a brand-new country. In this new country, immigrants were likely to encounter unfamiliar cultures and languages. Immigrants had varying degrees of difficulty getting accustomed to this new world.

Many immigrants lived in neighborhoods surrounded with people from the same country or with similar cultural backgrounds. This image features a Jewish neighborhood in New York City's Lower East Side in the early twentieth century.

6 Building a Life

Once they had entered the United States, immigrants had to deal with the same concerns of everyday life as citizens. They had to find homes, food, clothing, and jobs. They navigated unfamiliar neighborhoods and learned how to get around, shop, and communicate. They dealt with family life, school, and romance. Many of them did all this with no knowledge of English, the main language in the United States. All of them had to get used to new circumstances, laws, and freedoms. Additionally, some of them had to deal with the added difficulty of ethnic or racial prejudice. Some immigrants found the experience of jumping into a new and unfamiliar world to be an exciting adventure. For others, it was stressful and even frightening at times.

Established Communities

Several things helped immigrants with the shock of this new place. Many immigrants were linked together in networks of friends and relatives. These people who were already living in the States offered advice and help to those who came later. Immigrants found comfort in the ethnic neighborhoods and communities. Whether

Ole Bull, pictured here, was a world-famous violinist from Norway. He established a Norwegian ethnic colony in Pennsylvania. It failed within a year, however, because he did not secure legal ownership of the land and the land was not good for farming. Other ethnic colonies and neighborhoods were more successful.

in San Francisco's Chinatown, New York's Little Italy, or the Scandinavian towns of Minnesota, newcomers could speak in their native languages, buy familiar foods, and share their traditional holidays and customs with others from the same background.

Immigrants helped one another in more practical ways, too. Many ethnic groups formed self-help societies that collected dues. These societies used the money to offer loans or charitable gifts to members. Loans raised in this way helped many immigrants start their own businesses, go to college, or buy land.

A Continued Hope

As challenging as life in the United States could be, many immigrants accepted the challenges gladly. They had already given up so much and endured the journey to reach the United States, with all its risks and promises. They realized that their journey would continue long after they had stepped ashore.

Joseph Hollingsworth Celebrates a New Political System

Some immigrants were greatly pleased to find themselves living under political and social systems very different from those of their native countries. Early in the century of immigration, Joseph Hollingsworth wrote to an aunt and uncle in Yorkshire, England. He expressed his satisfaction with life in America and the country's political system.

> In this country ... [there is] no Royal Family to support ... The "President of the United States" is the highest Titled fellow ... He is chosen by the people ... The President when he makes a speech does not begin with "My Lords and Gentlemen" but with "Fellow Citizens" ...

KEY TERMS AND CONCEPTS

From Mother Jones's autobiography:

Ireland's freedom Ireland was fighting for freedom from the British Empire.

From Guri Endreden's letter:

deed A legal document usually regarding ownership of something.

heathen An individual who is not a Christian or who does not have religious beliefs, often used to refer to Native Americans.

savage An uncivilized person; a negative, offensive term used to refer to Native Americans.

—Quoted in Noel Rae, ed., *Witnessing America: The Library of Congress Book of Firsthand Accounts of Life in America 1600–1900* (Harmondsworth, UK: Penguin, 1996).

CONSIDER THIS

1. Why do you think Hollingsworth preferred the president to the royal family?

Mother Jones

Mary Harris was a child when she came to the United States from Ireland. When she grew up, she taught school and ran a dressmaking business in Chicago. Then, she married George Jones and settled with him in Memphis, Tennessee.

Mother Jones (1830–1930) was important in the struggle for workers' rights. She advocated for the United Mine Workers and cofounded the Industrial Workers of the World.

In 1867, her husband died from an epidemic, or widespread outbreak, of yellow fever. Afterward, she became involved in the struggle of American laborers to form unions, or groups of workers organized to protect the workers' rights. These labor unions would strike, or refuse to work as a form of protest, for better wages and working conditions. Until her death at the age of one hundred, Mother Jones, as she became known, was active in the labor movement. She arranged strikes, demonstrations, marches, and meetings in support of workers and their unions.

> I was born in the city of Cork, Ireland, in 1830. My people were poor. For generations they had fought for Ireland's freedom. Many of my folks have died in that struggle. My father, Richard Harris, came to America in 1835, and as soon as he had become an American citizen he sent for his family … Here I was brought up, but always as the child of an American citizen. Of that citizenship I have ever been proud …
>
> In 1867, a yellow fever epidemic swept Memphis. Its victims were mainly among the poor and the workers. The rich and the well-to-do fled the city …
>
> After the union had buried my husband, I got a permit to nurse the sufferers. This I did until the plague was stamped out.
>
> I returned to Chicago and went again into the dressmaking business … We worked for the aristocrats of Chicago, and I had ample opportunity to observe the luxury and extravagance of their lives.

> Often while sewing for the lords and barons who lived in magnificent houses on the Lake Shore Drive, I would look out of the plate glass windows and see the poor, shivering wretches, jobless and hungry, walking along the frozen lake front. The contrast of their condition with that of the tropical comfort of the people for whom I sewed was painful to me. My employers seemed neither to notice nor to care.
>
> —Mary Field Parton, ed., *The Autobiography of Mother Jones* (Chicago: Charles H. Keer & Co., 1925).

CONSIDER THIS

1. Do you think that Mother Jones's description of her Irish heritage is significant? How might her background have influenced her?
2. Based on the actions she mentions in this excerpt, what kind of a person do you think Jones was?

A Norwegian Pioneer

Some emigrants left their homelands to escape poverty, political oppression, or war. Many of those who immigrated to America's western states and territories, far from the cities, came in search of land that they could own and farm. Occasionally, these western settlers found themselves involved in a new kind of war. They were encountering the final stages of the frontier conflict. Tension had existed between settlers and Native Americans for more than two centuries. In 1866, pioneer immigrant Guri Endreden wrote from Minnesota to her mother and daughter in Norway. She wrote about how that conflict had affected her.

I do not seem to have been able to do so much to write to you, because during the time when the savages raged so fearfully here I was not able to think about anything except being murdered, with my whole family, by these terrible heathen. But God be praised, I escaped with my life, unharmed by them, and my four daughters also came through the danger unscathed.

Guri and Britha were carried off by the wild Indians, but they got a chance the next day to make their escape ... I myself wandered aimlessly around on my land with my youngest daughter, and I had to look on while they shot my precious husband dead, and in my sight my dear son Ole was shot through the shoulder ... We also found my oldest son Endre shot dead ... To be an eye-witness to these things and to see many others wounded and killed was almost too much for a poor woman; but God be thanked, I kept my life and my sanity, though all my movable property was torn away and stolen ...

I must also let you know that my daughter Gjaertru has land, which they received from the government under a law that has been passed, called in our language "the Homestead law," ... and after they have lived there five years they receive a deed and complete possession of the property and can sell it if they want to or keep it if they want to. She lives about twenty-four American miles [37 kilometers] from here and is doing well ...

The five men shown here, including George Engel (*bottom left*), were sentenced to death after the Haymarket Riot. Two others were sentenced to death as well, but their sentences were changed to life in prison.

KEY TERMS AND CONCEPTS

From George Engel's statement:

fare To travel.

for whom no table is set For whom there are no opportunities.

gallows A structure from which prisoners are hanged.

knawing Gnawing.

proletarian A working-class individual.

If you, my dear daughter, would come here, you could buy [my land], and then it would not be necessary to let it fall into the hands of strangers.

—Guri Endreden, letter, in Theodore C. Blegen, "Immigrant Women and the American Frontier," *Norwegian-American Studies*, Vol. 5 (Northfield, MN: The Norweigian-American Historical Association, 1930).

CONSIDER THIS

1. Can you think of reasons why the Native Americans might have attacked the Norwegian immigrants?
2. If you were the daughter addressed in the last paragraph, would you be interested in going to America and buying your mother's land?

George Engel's Address

Some immigrants felt that the United States was not perfect. They felt it needed improvement. In the late nineteenth and early twentieth centuries, immigrant workers made great contributions to the labor, reform, and progressive movements. These movements helped improve conditions for workers, slum dwellers, and the poor.

In addition to these movements, immigrants adopted diverse political ideologies, or systems of beliefs or ideas. Some immigrants adopted socialism, the theory that the government, not wealthy individuals, should own resources and manufacturing plants. Some who saw the great gap between rich and poor believed in anarchy. That theory called for the tearing down of existing political, social, and economic orders. The destruction of existing norms was in the hope that a more just society, with equal distribution of wealth, would somehow develop.

In 1886, there was an argument between anarchist demonstrators and police in Haymarket Square in Chicago. During said argument, someone threw a bomb. It killed seven policemen. Eight of the anarchist demonstrators were arrested. None of them, however, were accused of actually throwing the bomb. Instead, they were tried for spreading the ideas that had inspired the unknown bomb thrower. Seven were sentenced to death, and one was sent to prison. Each had a chance to present a statement to the court. The following statement is George Engel's. He was sentenced to death.

> When, in the year 1872, I left Germany because it had become impossible for me to gain there, by the labor of my hands, a livelihood such as man is worthy to enjoy—the introduction of machinery having ruined the smaller craftsmen and made the outlook for the future appear very dark to them—I concluded to fare

with my family to the land of America, the land that had been praised to me by so many as the land of liberty. On the occasion of my arrival at Philadelphia, on the 8th of January, 1873, my heart swelled with joy in the hope and in the belief that in the future I would live among free men, and in a free country. I made up my mind to become a good citizen of this country, and congratulated myself on having left Germany, and landed in this glorious republic. And I believe my past history will bear witness that I have ever striven to be a good citizen of this country. This is the first occasion of my standing before an American court, and on this occasion it is murder of which I am accused. And for what reason do I stand here? For what reasons am I accused of murder? The same that caused me to leave Germany—the poverty—the misery of the working classes.

And here, too, in this "free republic," in the richest country of the world, there are numerous proletarians for whom no table is set; who, as outcasts of society, stray joylessly through life. I have seen human beings gather their daily food from the garbage heaps of the streets, to quiet therewith their knawing hunger …

We see from the history of this country that the first colonists won their liberty only through force; that through force slavery was abolished, and just as the man who agitated against slavery in this country, had to ascend the gallows, so also must we. He who speaks for the workingman today must hang.

—From "Address of George Engel," *The Accused and the Accusers: The Famous Speeches of the Eight Chicago Anarchists in Court* (Chicago: Socialistic Publishing Co., n.d.).

CONSIDER THIS

1. How do you think Engel would define freedom?
2. To what past movements does Engel compare his own political action? Do you agree with his position?

Rocco Corresca's Padrone

Not all immigrants were generous and helpful toward their fellow countrymen and countrywomen. Once they found their footing in the United States and learned their way around, some immigrants took advantage of the less experienced. In 1902, a young immigrant from Italy described his relationship with Bartolo, his padrone. A padrone was a patron or protector for new immigrants, especially immigrants from Italy. The padrone would set an immigrant up with a job and housing. In return, he would receive a share of the immigrant's wages. As Corresca's account demonstrates, padrones often exploited their clients, or unfairly treated their clients in a way that benefited the padrones themselves. Padrones often subjected immigrants to difficult living and working conditions. Additionally, they often charged their clients extra money for basic needs like food and clothing.

Now and then I had heard things about America—that it was a far-off country where everybody was rich and that Italians went there and made plenty

This bilingual advertisement encouraged Yiddish-speaking Jewish immigrants to learn English with free classes.

of money, so that they could return to Italy and live in pleasure ever after. One day I met a young man who pulled out a handful of gold and told me he had made that in America in a few days ...

We came to Brooklyn to a wooden house ... full of Italians from Naples. Bartolo had a room on the third floor and there were fifteen men in the room, all boarding with Bartolo ...

Bartolo told us to go out and pick rags and get bottles. He gave us bags and hooks and showed us the ash barrels. On the streets where the fine houses are the people ... put out good things, like mattresses and umbrellas ... We brought all these to Bartolo and he made them new and sold them again on the sidewalk; but mostly we brought rags and bones ... Most of the men in our room worked at digging the sewer. Bartolo got them the work and they paid him about one quarter of their wages. Then he charged them for board and he bought the clothes for them, too ... [Bartolo] is now a very rich man. The men that were living with him had just come to the country and could not speak English ... Bartolo told us all that we must work for him and that if we did not the police would come and put us in prison.

He gave us very little money, and our clothes were some of those that we had found in the street. Still we had enough to eat and we had meat quite often, which we never had in Italy.

—Rocco Corresca, in "The Biography of a Bootblack," *Independent* 54, December 4, 1902.

CONSIDER THIS

1. How can you tell that Bartolo's treatment of the immigrants was unfair?
2. What would you do in Corresca's circumstances?

Carl Christian Jensen's Saga

Carl Christian Jensen came to the United States from Denmark in 1906. Years later, he wrote *An American Saga*. In his book, he describes some of the challenges of starting life over in a new land, including the challenge of learning a new language.

> I was a man and stronger than most men. Yet my second childhood began the day I entered my new country. I had to learn life over in a brand-new world. And I could not talk. My first desire was for chocolate drops, and I pointed my finger at them. My second was for fishing tackle, and I pointed my finger at a wrapped cord and heaved up an imaginary fish. I used baby talk. "Price?" I asked. And later in the day, "Vatsprice?" Saleswomen answered me with motherly grimaces.
>
> I never quite got over my second childhood. I doubt that any immigrant does—with his hasty, often harsh attuning to the new world.
>
> —Carl Christian Jensen, *An American Saga* (Boston: Little, Brown and Company, 1927).

CONSIDER THIS

1. Why do you think Jensen felt like a child again when he arrived in the United States?
2. What words or images does he use to support the theme of a "second childhood"?

Becoming an American

Many immigrants, like Jensen, had to endure this "second childhood" as they learned English and new ways of life in the United States. The American melting pot meant that lots of different cultures came together in cities like New York and San Francisco. Despite the variety of languages, cultures, and foods, all immigrants had to settle into life in the United States. Additionally, they had to develop their own American identities.

From Ellis Island, immigrants could see the Statue of Liberty, which served as a window into their new lives.

7

Americanization

Some immigrants came to America not to stay but merely to work for a while so that they could return to better lives in their countries of origin. The rate of return varied from time to time, depending upon economic conditions in the United States. It also varied among ethnic groups. Scandinavian immigrants, for example, seldom returned to their homelands. Large numbers of Chinese, British, Irish, and Italian immigrants, however, did return home. Still, the majority of those who immigrated to the United States came to stay.

Language

Most mastered the immediate challenges of finding housing and work. Those who didn't speak English either learned some English or used sign language or interpreters to communicate. In many immigrant families, children became the natural interpreters. If they were young when they arrived in the United States, they soon learned English in school or by playing with other kids. Children born in the United States often grew up speaking two languages. At school or in public places they spoke English, while at home they and their parents talked in the language of the old country.

The Question of American Identity

Children raised questions of identity for some immigrants. People who came to America felt two conflicting desires. On one hand, many immigrants strongly wanted to assimilate, or integrate, into mainstream American culture and society. They wanted to be regarded as Americans, not foreigners. If they couldn't completely make the transition, they hoped that their children could.

On the other hand, however, many immigrants also feared losing their cultural heritage. They saw how easy it was to fall out of touch with family and friends they had left behind. They wondered whether they were leaving behind other things as well, like languages, customs, or religious practices. In response to these fears, they founded cultural organizations and schools to preserve these traditions and pass them on to younger generations. Battle lines were often drawn in immigrant households between parents who feared that their children or grandchildren were becoming too American and young people who were impatient with extra language classes and Old World customs.

In the end, each immigrant decided for himself or herself what being American meant. Today, the children, grandchildren, and great-grandchildren of those who came during the century of immigration continue to seek a balance between blending in and maintaining an ethnic identity. By doing both, immigrants past and present have made American society unique.

"Promising Opportunities": The First German American Senator's Story

As a twenty-year-old student, Carl Schurz took part in a revolutionary movement that tried to bring a republican government to Germany in 1848–1849. The movement failed. Afterward, many of the idealistic revolutionaries, including Schurz, immigrated to the United States to escape punishment. Schurz became a lawyer and a supporter of Abraham Lincoln and the Republican Party, which formed a few years before Lincoln was elected to the presidency. He fought on the Union side in the Civil War, reaching the rank of major general.

After the war, Schurz settled in Missouri. In 1869, his fellow citizens elected him to the US Senate, where he remained for six years. He was then secretary of the interior, a position that is responsible for the conservation of the country's land and natural resources, from 1877 to 1881. Schurz was the first German American to serve his new country as senator and cabinet member. Eventually, he wrote about his life. The first of these passages describes a speech Schurz made about democracy in Boston in 1859.

> The old-fashioned hall was filled with a typical Boston audience. Here I was to strike my blow at Nativism and the politics of sly tricks and petty scheming. My speech seemed to have a good effect. I spoke with great passion and mainly emphasized the concept which was my guiding principle throughout my entire political career in America: the important part which this republic has to play in the progress of humanity toward democratic forms of government, and the resulting enormous responsibility of the American people to the entire civilized world. It may sound

> unlikely and almost ridiculously presumptuous to assert that foreign-born Americans can be more impassioned and sincere in their patriotism for America than many native-born ones are, and yet my experience showed that to be the case.

In the second of these two passages, Schurz describes how it felt to take his Senate seat. He was honored and excited for the privilege to serve his new country.

> I clearly remember my feelings upon taking my seat: I was all choked up. I had attained the highest public office I could ever have dreamed of. I was still young; I had just turned forty. Only a little more than sixteen years had passed since I landed in America as a homeless refugee, rescued from the great shipwreck of the revolutionary movement in Europe. At that time the American people took me in with heartwarming hospitality; they opened all the many promising opportunities the New World had to offer, as generously to me as to their native children. And now I was a member of the highest legislative body of the greatest Republic. Would I ever be able to repay my debt of gratitude to this country and justify all the honors heaped upon me?
>
> —Rüdiger Werisch, ed., Carl Schurz, *Revolutionary and Statesman: His Life in Personal and Official Documents, with Illustrations* (Munich, Germany: Heinz Moos Verlag, 1979).

KEY TERMS AND CONCEPTS

From Carl Schurz's book:

attain To achieve.

refugee A person forced to leave their country because of war, persecution, or natural disaster.

From the *Information for Immigration* booklet:

availing Using or taking advantage of.

CONSIDER THIS

1. Why might Schurz have felt that foreign-born Americans were often more passionately patriotic than native-born ones?
2. Do you think that an immigrant from China would have been met with the same "heartwarming hospitality" and "promising opportunities" as Schurz?

Questions and Answers: Information for Immigrants

In 1908, the Bureau of Immigration and Naturalization issued a booklet called *Information for Immigrants Concerning the United States: Its Opportunities, Government, and Institutions*. The booklet was prepared by the National Society of the Sons of the American Revolution. It was an organization of men who could trace their ancestry to someone who had fought in the Revolutionary War (1775–1783). The booklet provided answers to seven questions asked by "most of those who come to the United States." Among the questions were, "Is it or is it not true that anyone can become rich in this country?" and "What is the religion of this country?" A portion of the booklet's text follows.

> The person who leaves the land in which he was born, and goes to another to make his home, wants to know the truth about a number of things in the land to which he goes. To give such information this is prepared, not by any set of men who are interested in availing themselves of your labor or seeking to get your money, but by a society which has for its object the teaching to all of a love of country, and is composed of the descendants of the men to whom the United States owes its existence as a distinct country ...
>
> This is a great country to which you have come. It extends from where the snow and ice never entirely melt on the north to where frost is never known on the south, from an ocean in the east 3,000 miles [4,825 km] to an ocean on the west. It has great lakes and rivers, high mountains, fertile plains and valleys. There are great stores of coal, iron, and natural oil. Almost every variety of fruits and grains is found in large quantities, and great mills and factories

> manufacture everything that is necessary for comfort. This is the land to which you have come. May you be worthy of it.
>
> —*Information for Immigrants Concerning the United States: Its Opportunities, Government, and Institutions* (Washington, DC: Government Printing Office, 1908).

CONSIDER THIS

1. How do the booklet's authors set themselves apart from other sources of information? Why do you think they do so?
2. When the authors ask immigrants to "be worthy" of their new home, what do you think they mean?

"My America": A Bulgarian Immigrant's Choice

In ethnic colonies, people were surrounded by others with a shared background and memories of the old country. These communities felt safe and comforting for many immigrants. It was especially comforting for those who were bothered by the sense of being strangers in a strange land.

Stoyan Christowe, however, rejected such a life. He came to the United States from Bulgaria in 1911. Christowe spent several years living in a Bulgarian neighborhood in an eastern city. Then he went to Montana and studied English. That experience gave him a new vision of his future in America.

> The language was full of mysteries and adventure. Every new word I learned brought to me something new and exciting. Since my contact with America

While some immigrants chose to live in ethnic neighborhoods, like the Italian one featured here, others, like Stoyan Christowe, rejected the idea.

and its people was necessarily limited, through the language I sought to link myself with them. If I mastered the speech, I felt certain I would come nearer attaining my American ideal. I knew then as I know now that the language was the passport to my America.

The track hands who came to Montana for the summers and returned East for the winters to live in colonies made up of their own countrymen had little in common with America. Many had been in America ten years and still they were strangers in this country. They thought old-country thoughts, spoke only their native tongues. All of them were interested in making money, and that was their only contact with America. I was fortunate to see the tragedy of these people. And I did not want the same thing to happen to me.

I was now, after five years, on the eve of a second journey to America. I was ready and eager to return to the East, but not to the colony. America was not there. My America was elsewhere. No train or steamship could take me to it. I alone must find it.

—Stoyan Christowe, *This Is My Country,* 1938, quoted in Frances Cavanah, ed., *We Came to America: An Anthology* (Philadelphia: Macrae Smith Co., 1954).

CONSIDER THIS

1. Christowe speaks of making "a second voyage to America." What does he mean?
2. Why does Christowe describe the situation of the immigrant workers he saw as a "tragedy"?

Ernesto Galarza: Proud and Not Ashamed

Ernesto Galarza was born in 1905 in the town of Jalcocotán, Mexico. His family immigrated to California when he was eight years old. At once, he was plunged into school with American-born children as well as other young immigrants from Japan, Italy, Portugal, Korea, and Yugoslavia. Years later, he described his childhood in *Barrio Boy*. The book is about his experiences growing up in a Latin community within an American city. It describes his elementary school and the educator whose task was "the Americanization of Mexican me."

> Miss Hopley and her teachers never let us forget why we were at Lincoln ... The school was not so much a melting-pot as a griddle where Miss Hopley and her helpers warmed knowledge into us and roasted racial hatreds out of us ...
>
> Making us into Americans did not mean scrubbing away what made us originally foreign. The teachers called us as our parents did, or as close as they could ... No one was ever scolded ... for speaking in his native tongue ... Encarnación acted out how boys learned to fish in the Philippines. I astounded the third grade with the story of my travels on a stagecoach ... Miss Hopley herself had a way of

> expressing wonder over these matters ... It was easy for me to feel that becoming a proud American, as she said we should, did not mean feeling ashamed of being a Mexican.
>
> —Ernesto Galarza, *Barrio Boy* (South Bend, IN: University of Notre Dame Press, 1971)

CONSIDER THIS

1. Do you think that Miss Hopley's approach to educating multicultural children was the standard for her day?
2. How does young Ernesto's experience of school compare with your own?

A Note on the Principle of "Americanization"

In the early years of the twentieth century, a New York City publishing company produced a series of books called *Americanization Studies*. Each book dealt with a different aspect of immigrant life in the United States. The publishers added a note to each volume that explained the principle of "Americanization" upon which the series was based.

> Americanization in this study has been considered as the union of native and foreign born in all the most fundamental relationships and activities of our national life. For Americanization is the uniting of new with native-born Americans in fuller common understanding and appreciation to secure by means of self-government the highest welfare of all. Such Americanization should perpetuate no

KEY TERMS AND CONCEPTS

From *Americanization Studies*:

commonweal The well-being of the public.

perpetuate To continue indefinitely.

unchangeable political, domestic, and economic regime delivered once for all to the fathers, but a growing and broadening of national life, inclusive of the best wherever found. With all our rich heritages, Americanism will develop best through a mutual giving and taking of contributions from both newer and older Americans in the interest of the commonweal. This study has followed such an understanding of Americanization.

—Kate Holladay Claghorn, *The Immigrant's Day in Court* (New York: Harper & Brothers, 1923).

CONSIDER THIS

1. How does this view of immigration compare with that of Israel Zangwill in *The Melting-Pot*?
2. If you were a new immigrant, how would you feel about this definition of Americanization?

"Let's Go to America": An Issei Woman's Story

During the second half of the twentieth century, immigrant studies became a recognized field of research. Historians examined the causes and effects of the century of immigration. Scholars also collected and published old interviews and letters that shone light on the lives and experiences of immigrants. Additionally, some immigrants wrote their own stories.

One scholar, Akemi Kikumura, wanted to investigate the lives of Japanese women who had come to the United States early in the century. She told the story of one such woman in *Through Harsh Winters: The Life of a Japanese Immigrant Woman*. Kikumura explained, "This book was written out of respect and admiration for these courageous women who had managed to transform hardship, suffering, and despair into determination, understanding, and hope." Kikumura wrote the book in order to both tell these women's stories and learn more about her cultural heritage. She wrote about her mother's experiences as a way to "tell a story about an issei woman's experience in America." The term "issei" refers to someone who was born in Japan but immigrated to the United States.

In writing about one immigrant's life, Kikumura explored her family history. Here, her mother describes how she persuaded her husband, Kikumura's father, to come to America.

> I kept coaxing Papa, "Let's go to America." ... I had consented to marriage with Papa because I had the dream of seeing America. I didn't care for him much ... I could have married a real good person in Japan, but I wanted to see America ...

> Grandfather Tanaka said to us, "... America is not such a good place and besides you may never be able to get back, so don't go." My mother wasn't happy that we were leaving, either. She said, if we stayed, she would give us the noodle shop ... and we could run it together. But I kept urging Papa, "Let's go to America." ... We decided to go for a short while, make enough money for our trip, then return home. With that thought in mind, ... we left Yokohama on the *Korea Maru*, bound for America. It was January, 1923.
>
> —Akemi Kikumura, *Through Harsh Winters: The Life of a Japanese Immigrant Woman* (Novato, CA: Chandler & Sharp, 1981).

CONSIDER THIS

1. How would you describe Kikumura's mother?
2. Are there immigrants in your family or among your family friends? Do you know their stories?

More Stories

Kikumura's mother entered the country just a year before the Johnson-Reed Act, which ended the century of immigration, was passed. After the act went ino effect, immigration to the United States was reduced dramatically.

The story of American immigration did not end, though. During the 1940s, when the United States was engaged in World War II, immigration laws began to loosen slightly. The Immigration and Nationality Act of 1965, also known as the Hart-Celler Act, ended the restrictive quotas and launched a new, much more open era in American immigration. Since 1965, immigrants from all

This political cartoon depicts how people against immigration were children of immigrants themselves.

parts of the world have been able to enter the United States in much greater numbers than between 1924 and 1965.

Even still, responses to immigration have swayed between open arms of welcome and closed gates of rejection at different points in US history. The immigration debate continues into the twenty-first century as citizens and politicians weigh issues of security and national identity. Responses are also affected by the economic costs and benefits of immigrants and the question of how to deal with illegal immigration.

For instance, in 2017, President Donald Trump issued Executive Order 13769, called "Protecting the Nation from Foreign Terrorist Entry into the United States." An executive order is a set of instructions issued by the president. Trump created this order to ban emigration from Iran, Iraq, Libya, Somalia, Sudan, Syria, and Yemen, countries with predominately Muslim populations. He was concerned that people from these nations might commit terrorist acts in the United States. The order was later revised, replacing some of Muslim-majority countries with non-Muslim nations such as North Korea and Venezuela.

Many people criticized this executive order as religious persecution. Since the Constitution protects people from religious-based persecution, the order faced challenges in the US court system, eventually reaching the US Supreme Court. In June 2018, in a 5–4 vote, the Supreme Court upheld, or ruled constitutional, President Trump's immigration ban. Although many conservatives celebrate the ruling, liberals are concerned that the US government is repeating mistakes of its past. This immigration ban, however, is just one of the many hotly debated immigration-related topics that have arisen over this country's history.

As immigration continues, there will continue to be responses from native-born Americans. In addition to those responses, it will continue to be important to look at the stories of those who bravely left their countries to start a new life in the United States.

On January 26, 2018, the one-year anniversary of President Trump's immigration ban, activists rallied and protested.

CHRONOLOGY

1790 Congress passes the first national citizenship law, the Naturalization Act, which allows a "free white person" to become a citizen after living in the country for two years.

1803 The British Parliament passes the Passenger Vessels Act, which attempts to improve the conditions on ships crossing the Atlantic. The Louisiana Purchase doubles the size of United States and opens land to European immigrants.

1819 The federal government passes the Steerage Act, or the Manifest of Immigrants Act, which limits the number of passengers and improves conditions on ships arriving in the United States.

1820 The federal government starts keeping immigration records.

1855 The federal government passes the Carriage of Passengers Act, replacing the Steerage Act of 1819, which defines conditions for arrival of immigrants by sea. Castle Garden, the first official station for receiving immigrants, opens in New York City.

1882 The Chinese Exclusion Act prohibits the immigration of Chinese laborers for ten years.

1883 Emma Lazarus's poem "The New Colossus" celebrates America's open door to immigration.

1886 The Statue of Liberty opens and is officially dedicated.

1891 The Office of the Superintendent of Immigration, later called the Bureau of Immigration, is established within the federal government to oversee immigration, taking control away from individual states.

1892 The federal government opens the Ellis Island station in New York Harbor to receive immigrants.

1908 Israel Zangwill's play *The Melting Pot* celebrates the United States as a land of new possibilities for immigrants.

1910 The federal government opens the Angel Island receiving station in San Francisco.

1917 The Immigration Act of 1917 sets a literacy standard.

1924 Congress passes Johnson-Reed Act, limiting immigration and setting quotas for immigration based on national origin.

GLOSSARY

anarchy A political philosophy that opposes all forms of organized government.

Chinese Exclusion Act This federal law, effective in 1882, prohibited immigration of Chinese laborers for ten years. The act was later extended; it was not repealed until 1943.

emigrant Someone who emigrates or has emigrated.

emigrate To leave one's native land in order to live somewhere else.

exile Someone separated by necessity from his or her homeland; the state of living apart from one's homeland.

immigrant Someone who immigrates or has immigrated.

immigrate To enter a new country with the goal of living there.

Johnson-Reed Act This law, also known as the Immigration Act of 1924, set quotas on the number of immigrants from each country. The passage of it marked the end of the century of immigration.

legislator A person who makes laws, or a member of a legislative body.

nativism A movement that opposed immigration on the grounds that it was harmful to "native-born" Americans.

naturalization The process through which someone becomes a citizen of a nation other than the country in which he or she was born.

occupation The act of taking over or staying in a place, often by a military.

persecute To treat someone negatively because of a person's race, politics, or religion.

prejudice An often negative opinion not based on fact or experiences.

quota A set number or amount; a limit.

republic A country with elected representatives as opposed to a king or queen.

slum An area inhabited by poor people.

steerage The part of a ship that has accommodations for those with the cheapest tickets.

strike The refusal to work as a form of protest.

union A group of workers organized to protect the workers' rights.

FURTHER INFORMATION

Books

Kravitz, Danny. *In the Shadow of Lady Liberty: Immigrant Stories from Ellis Island.* US Immigration in the 1900s. North Mankato, MN: Capstone Press, 2016.

Nazario, Sonia. *Enrique's Journey: The True Story of a Boy Determined to Reunite with His Mother, Adapted for Young People*. New York: Delacorte Press, 2013.

Osborne, Linda Barret. *This Land Is Our Land: A History of American Immigration.* New York: Abrams, 2016.

Tan, Shaun. *The Arrival.* New York: Arthur A. Levine Books, 2007

Websites

From Haven to Home: 350 Years of Jewish Life in America
https://www.loc.gov/exhibits/haventohome

This Library of Congress website provides an overview of a 2004 exhibit about the Jewish experience in America.

On the Water: Ocean Crossings
http://americanhistory.si.edu/onthewater/exhibition/5_1.html

This Smithsonian website provides a glimpse into life on the ocean for the millions of immigrants that arrived via ships.

The University of Minnesota's Immigration History Research Center
http://www.umn.edu/ihrc

This website contains facts about immigration and genealogy in the United States, as well as links to many other sites.

Videos

The Immigration of the United States
https://www.youtube.com/watch?v=lBJcqxI7kas

This video provides an overview of immigration, starting with the Native Americans who migrated to the Americas from Asia.

Island of Hope – Island of Tears
https://www.youtube.com/watch?v=qh5CWbTDsuQ

This video provides background about immigration from Europe to the United States through Ellis Island.

Organizations

Angel Island Immigration Station Foundation
870 Market Street, Suite 941
San Francisco, CA 94102
(415) 658-7691
Website: https://www.historymuseum.ca

This foundation raises awareness about immigration to America across the Pacific Ocean. It provides additional primary sources from people who immigrated and educational resources related to immigration.

The Center for Immigration Studies
1629 K Street NW, Suite 600
Washington, DC 20006
(202) 466-8185
Website: http://www.cis.org

The Center for Immigration Studies focuses on current immigration-related news and opinions. It also provides concise background information on other topics, including the history of immigration.

The Statue of Liberty—Ellis Island Foundation, Inc.
Ellis Island National Museum of Immigration
Statue of Liberty National Monument
New York, NY 10004
(212) 561-4500
Website: http://www.libertyellisfoundation.org

This foundation manages the immigration museum on Ellis Island as well as the Statue of Liberty Museum on Liberty Island. The website provides information about family histories, photos, details about immigrant experiences, and a searchable database of family names.

Tenement Museum
103 Orchard Street,
New York, NY 10002
(877) 975-3786
Website: http://www.tenement.org

This museum provides an interpretation of the stories of immigrants who settled in Manhattan's Lower East Side. In addition to tours of tenements, rundown and often overcrowded apartment buildings, the museum also has neighborhood tours, lectures, and resources to help visitors learn more about the lives of New York City immigrants in the nineteenth and twentieth centuries. It also provides language courses for today's immigrants.

United States Citizenship and Immigration Services
20 Massachusetts Ave NW
Washington, DC 20529
(800) 375-5283
Website: http://uscis.gov

This federal organization is a branch of the US Department of Homeland Security. It is responsible for the administrative and legal execution of processes related to immigration and naturalization.

Young Center for Immigrant Children's Rights
6020 S University Ave
Chicago, IL 60637
(773) 702-9560
Website: https://www.theyoungcenter.org

This organization is dedicated to protecting and advocating for immigrant children, especially those who arrived to the United States alone.

INDEX

Page numbers in **boldface** refer to images.

INDEX

ABOUT THE AUTHORS

Chet'la Sebree is a writer, editor, and researcher from the Mid-Atlantic. She has received degrees in English and writing from the University of Richmond and American University. She has worked on several books about US history, including the Courting History series for Cavendish Square Publishing.

Rebecca Stefoff is the author of numerous historical nonfiction books, including a historical atlas series and a book about colonial life. She has also adapted Ronald Takaki's prizewinning history of Asian immigration and the Asian American experience, *Strangers from a Different Shore*. She currently lives in Portland, Oregon.